EUGENE O'NEILL
THE ICEMAN COMETH

Introduction by
Christine Dymkowski

ROYAL NATIONAL THEATRE
London

N H **B**

NICK HERN BOOKS

The Iceman Cometh first published in this edition in 1993 jointly by the Royal National Theatre, London, and Nick Hern Books Limited, 14 Larden Road, London W3 7ST

Reprinted 1995, 1998 (twice)

First published in Great Britain by Jonathan Cape in 1947
Copyright © 1940 by Eugene O'Neill

Introduction, Biographical Sketch of Eugene O'Neill and List of Produced Plays Copyright © 1993 by Christine Dymkowski

Cover photograph of Eugene O'Neill by courtesy of the Raymond Mander & Joe Mitcheson Theatre Collection

Set in Baskerville by Edna A. Moore, ⚘ Tek Art, Addiscombe, Surrey
Printed and bound in England By Athenæum Press Ltd, Gateshead, Tyne & Wear

British Library Cataloguing in Publication Data: a catalogue record for this book is available from the British Library

ISBN 1 85459 143 6

EUGENE O'NEILL

Born in New York City in 1888, son of a well-known actor, Eugene O'Neill spent a year at Princeton University (1906) before signing on as a seaman and travelling widely. Following a period in a sanatorium recovering from TB, he wrote his first play, *A Wife for a Life*. In 1916 he joined the Provincetown Players, who produced the first of his plays to be staged, *Bound East for Cardiff*, as well as other early work. His Broadway debut came in 1920 with *Beyond the Horizon*, which also won him a Pulitzer Prize.

The next fourteen years saw the premieres of some twenty new plays, including *The Emperor Jones* (1920), *Anna Christie* (1921), which won a second Pulitzer Prize, *The Hairy Ape* (1922), *All God's Chillun Got Wings* (1924), *Desire Under the Elms* (1924), *The Great God Brown* (1926), *Strange Interlude* (1928), which won another Pulitzer, *Mourning Becomes Electra* (1931), a trilogy reworking the *Oresteia*, *Ah! Wilderness* (1933) and *Days Without End* (1933), after which thirteen years elapsed with no new play reaching the stage, though he continued writing. Two more plays were produced during his lifetime: *The Iceman Cometh* in 1946, though written in 1939, and *A Moon for the Misbegotten* in 1947, though it only reached Broadway ten years later, after his death in 1953.

Plays staged posthumously include *Long Day's Journey into Night* (1956), which won a fourth Pulitzer, *A Touch of the Poet* (1958) and *More Stately Mansions* (1962). He was three times married, his third wife, Carlotta Monterey, surviving him. In 1936 he became the first American dramatist to win the Nobel Prize for Literature.

In the same series

Anna Christie & The Emperor Jones
The Hairy Ape & All God's Chillun Got Wings
Long Day's Journey into Night
A Moon for the Misbegotten
Mourning Becomes Electra
Strange Interlude
A Touch of the Poet

In preparation

Desire Under the Elms & The Great God Brown
Ah! Wilderness

Biographical Sketch of Eugene O'Neill (1888–1953)

'Some day James O'Neill will best be known as the father of
Eugene O'Neill': so Eugene himself frequently boasted
throughout 1912. The claim struck those who heard it not with a
sense of the young man's prescience but of his presumption.
Nothing in his life so far had given any indication that in less
than a decade he would be a playwright to reckon with, shaking
up the American theatre and shaping a new American drama.
Instead, he seemed more likely to become one of the pipe-
dreamers who eternally inhabit Harry Hope's no-chance saloon in
his own *The Iceman Cometh*.

Born on 16 October 1888, to the respected and accomplished
actor James O'Neill and his wife Ella Quinlan O'Neill, Eugene
was to find his family an overwhelming force in his life and to
make it the almost constant subject of his plays. He was the
O'Neills' third son: the eldest, Jamie, had been born ten years
before; a second son, Edmund, had followed five years later. Life
was not easy for the O'Neills and their two young children; James
was already touring the country in *Monte Cristo*, the vehicle that
would spell both his financial success and his artistic defeat (he
succumbed to popular demand and played the role 4000 times
between 1883 and 1912). Ella, convent-educated and proper,
loved her husband but felt she had married beneath her; she
never took to James's theatrical life or to his theatrical friends.
However, the couple could not bear to be parted, and Ella, with
great reluctance, frequently left the children in the care of her
mother to join her husband on the road. Early in 1885, on one of
these occasions, Jamie contracted measles and disobeyed
instructions to stay away from his brother; Edmund became ill
and died.

Such family history might in another case seem irrelevant, but
it is crucial for an understanding of Eugene O'Neill and of his
work. Ella did not want any more children after Edmund's death,
but James, convinced that it would help solace her, persuaded
her to have another. The result was a family tragedy that
blighted all four lives, and not least the new baby, Eugene. In an
attempt to counteract the pain of an exceedingly difficult birth,
Ella was unwittingly precipitated into the morphine addiction

from which she would suffer for the next twenty-six years. James, Jamie, and Eugene were greatly affected by Ella's distraction and withdrawal from reality, but Jamie and Eugene endured a private hell of guilt: Jamie for inadvertently killing the brother whose loss had had such drastic consequences, and Eugene for having been born at all.

Fifteen when he learned of his mother's addiction, Eugene no longer had to fear the mental illness he had up till then suspected he would inherit; the truth, however, was worse. Although summers were spent at the family's home in New London, Connecticut, their haphazard existence in a succession of hotels while James was on tour had already given Eugene a sense of rootlessness that plagued him all his life. Now, guilty that his birth had effected such misery, he developed a deep sense of unbelonging that at times manifested itself as a death-wish. He rejected his parents' Catholicism and, under Jamie's influence, began to drink and to visit brothels. Both Jamie and Eugene, displacing their anger, blamed their father for their mother's condition, accusing him of hiring a 'quack' to attend Ella at Eugene's birth. In fact, even reputable doctors at that time prescribed morphine, and in doses so low that addiction was by no means inevitable.

Eugene entered Princeton in 1906, but only stayed a year, having spent most of his time drinking, cutting classes, and following his own reading interests. It was at this time that he discovered Nietzsche's *Thus Spake Zarathustra*, which together with the works of Strindberg, became his personal bible. After leaving Princeton, he worked for a short time in a New York office job arranged by his father. In the city's Greenwich Village, Hell's Kitchen, and Tenderloin districts, he began to frequent the dives he would immortalise in many of his plays and also began to write poetry. O'Neill remained a heavy drinker for years, though he never drank while writing; in 1926 he gave up alcohol completely, lapsing only a few times thereafter.

Wishing to escape from a romantic entanglement with Kathleen Jenkins, O'Neill let his father arrange for him to join a mining expedition in Honduras in October 1909. Nevertheless, because Kathleen was pregnant, he agreed to marry her shortly before his departure. Having contracted malaria after a few months in Central America, Eugene returned to the US and, without visiting his wife and new-born son (Eugene O'Neill, Jr.), joined his father's company on tour, checking tickets. Shortly afterwards, in June 1910, O'Neill boarded the *Charles Racine*, a Norwegian windjammer, as a working passenger on its two-month voyage to

Buenos Aires. O'Neill loved the sea – he was throughout his life a keen and able swimmer – and now had the chance to experience a sailing life first-hand; it was an experience he would exploit in many of his early plays.

O'Neill remained in Argentina for several months, occasionally working but mainly living as a down-and-out; he sailed back to New York in March 1911 on the S.S. *Ikala*, this time as a member of the crew. He stayed in New York long enough to arrange for a divorce, living in an alcoholic haze at a downtown bar and flophouse called Jimmy-the-Priest's. In July, he signed onto the S.S. *New York* as an ordinary seaman for its voyage to Southampton; he returned in August on the S.S. *Philadelphia* as an able-bodied seaman, a qualification of which he was to remain proud for the rest of his life. Resuming his destitute way of life at Jimmy-the-Priest's – though he regularly attended the performances of Dublin's Abbey Players, who were visiting New York – O'Neill sank progressively into a depression that in January 1912 culminated in a suicide attempt. When he had sufficiently recovered, he rejoined his father's company for a few months, this time taking on small acting roles.

1912 seemed to mark a watershed in O'Neill's life, as evidenced both by his boasting of future fame and by his setting of many of his most autobiographical plays in that year. Moving to New London, Connecticut, in the summer, he worked as a reporter for the *Telegraph*, continued to write poetry, and developed a mild case of tuberculosis. By the end of the year, he was at the Gaylord Farm Sanatorium, where he was to remain for six months. During that time he decided to become a playwright.

Returning to New London in summer 1913 and boarding with the Rippins, a local family, he began to write one-act plays based on his own experiences. O'Neill's father subsidised their publication as *Thirst and Other One Act Plays* in August 1914, and the following September O'Neill enrolled in Professor George Pierce Baker's famous play-writing course at Harvard. Although he did not particularly distinguish himself in the class, his disdain for easy formulaic success made clear his ambition to be an original dramatist.

After his year at Harvard, O'Neill returned to New York and became somewhat involved in the political and intellectual life of Greenwich Village, frequenting the Golden Swan saloon, familiarly known as the 'Hell Hole'. He submitted some plays to the adventurous Washington Square Players, who had recently formed in reaction to the glib, commercial offerings of Broadway; however, the Players were not so adventurous as to stage any of O'Neill's works.

His first real theatrical opportunity came in June 1916 when he accompanied his friend Terry Carlin to Provincetown, at the tip of Massachusetts's Cape Cod. Then, as now, Provincetown boasted a flourishing artists' colony each summer. The previous year, the writer Susan Glaspell, her husband Jig Cook, and other vacationing Greenwich Village friends had staged an impromptu production, marking the birth of what would become the Provincetown Players. When O'Neill arrived in Provincetown, the group were desperately short of plays for their new season. O'Neill offered them *Bound East for Cardiff*, which premiered on 28 July 1916, the first-ever performance of an O'Neill play. His work with the Players also led to his involvement in Greenwich Village's radical circle, which included John Reed, Louise Bryant, Mabel Dodge, and Floyd Dell, among others.

The Provincetown Players' success was such that in September 1916 they moved operations to Greenwich Village, acquiring a base on Macdougal Street, which at O'Neill's suggestion was named the Playwrights' Theatre. During the group's eight subscription seasons between 1916 and 1922, O'Neill had ample opportunity to experiment without regard to commercial considerations. For example, *The Emperor Jones*, staged by the Provincetown Players in November 1920, not only had an African-American for its protagonist but was also considerably shorter than standard length. Despite its unconventionality, the play marked the group's first popular success: following its scheduled performances at the Playwrights' Theatre, it moved uptown to Broadway for an unlimited run. When the original Provincetown Players disbanded, O'Neill, together with the designer Robert Edmond Jones and the critic-producer Kenneth Macgowan, founded the Experimental Theatre, Inc., in 1923. The triumvirate ran the Playwrights' Theatre, now renamed the Provincetown Playhouse, from 1923–25 and the Greenwich Village Theatre from 1924–26.

The Provincetown Players' success with *The Emperor Jones* was not O'Neill's first theatrical triumph. *Beyond the Horizon*, which opened at the Morosco Theatre on Broadway in February 1920, was greeted by extremely favourable reviews, transferred for an extended run, and brought O'Neill his first Pulitzer Prize (the second drama award in the prize's four-year history). This success was quickly followed by another: *Anna Christie* opened in November 1921 and brought him a second Pulitzer. He was to win the award twice more, for *Strange Interlude* in 1928 and posthumously in 1956 for *Long Day's Journey into Night*, a record that has not been matched.

By the time of his early success, O'Neill's personal life had undergone considerable change: married for a second time, to the writer Agnes Boulton, he had become a father again with the birth of Shane Rudraighe O'Neill on 30 October 1919 (his last child, Oona, who later married Charlie Chaplin, was born on 14 May 1925). His father had died in August 1920, having lived long enough to see his younger son succeed; in the year prior to his death, Eugene had finally recognised his father's long-standing forbearance and support and had become friendly with him. Ironically, O'Neill's own neediness so dominated his life that he could never be a father to his own children, who all suffered the neglect for which O'Neill had bitterly and unfairly resented his own father. Eugene Jr. committed suicide at the age of forty, and Shane was for many years a heroin addict.

Within three years of his father's death, O'Neill was the sole survivor of his original family: his mother died of a brain tumour in February 1922, and Jamie had drunk himself to death by November 1923. Their deaths freed O'Neill to explore the dark side of his family life, which he proceeded to do in plays as diverse (and variously successful) as *All God's Chillun Got Wings*, *Dynamo*, *Long Day's Journey into Night*, and *A Moon for the Misbegotten*. Further change was in store: in 1927 O'Neill left Agnes Boulton for Carlotta Monterey, who became his third wife in July 1929. Misogynist, desirous of a mother, unable to separate love from hate, O'Neill had difficult relationships with women. He found his own guilt at his desertion of Agnes too difficult to deal with, and, as he later did with his children, manufactured grievances against her. His third marriage fulfilled his desire that his wife should be completely dedicated to his own interests, but it was a stormy one with cruelty on both sides.

O'Neill was quintessentially an autobiographical playwright: many of his protagonists are recognisable O'Neill figures, sharing the playwright's own lean build and dark deep-set eyes. All of his experiences found their way onto the stage, from the sea-going life depicted in early one-act plays like *Bound East for Cardiff* to his ambivalence about parenthood in *The First Man* to his Strindbergian view of marital relations in *Welded*. This need to depict, explain, and justify himself had considerable ramifications for his role as a playwright: he could not really regard theatre as the collaborative activity it so patently is. Time and again. O'Neill lamented the process of staging his plays, complaining that the ideal play he had seen in his head never existed in production. Whereas playwrights generally welcome the new life that actors and directors bring to their work, O'Neill saw it as a betrayal. So strongly did he feel this that he virtually never went to any productions of his plays, only attending rehearsals in order to advise and to cut when necessary.

In addition, his personal investment in what he wrote often blinded him to its deficiencies: he could be convinced that inferior works like *Welded*, *Dynamo*, and *Days Without End* were undervalued and misjudged. For example, while *Dynamo* ostensibly focused on the relationship between humankind, machines, and religion, it was really O'Neill's working out of his ambivalent relationship to his mother: small wonder that it made more sense to O'Neill than to the critics. However, at his best, O'Neill was able to transmute his personal experiences into the most powerful of dramas, as he does in works like *Long Day's Journey into Night* and *The Iceman Cometh.*

Although he wrote essentially to please himself and to exorcise his private demons (as early as 1924 he claimed that 'Writing is my vacation from living'), O'Neill was genuinely interested in stretching American drama beyond the narrow confines it had so far inhabited. His experiments were many: trying to make the audience share a character's hallucination in *Where the Cross is Made*, extending the audience's endurance by writing four- and five-hour long plays, using set location schematically in *Beyond the Horizon*, incorporating expressionistic elements in *The Hairy Ape*, masking the characters in *The Great God Brown*, modernising the use of the aside in *Strange Interlude*, developing a modern equivalent for the Greek sense of tragedy in *Desire Under the Elms* and *Mourning Becomes Electra*, creating an ambitious play-cycle detailing a critical history of America through the story of one family in *A Tale of Possessors Self-Dispossessed* (of which only *A Touch of the Poet* was completed to his satisfaction).

Although his achievements won him the Nobel Prize for literature in 1936, in the last years of his life O'Neill was something of a has-been. He had suffered for years from a hand tremor, caused by a rare degenerative disease of the cerebellum that attacks the motor system, which made writing increasingly difficult; by 1943, it had become impossible. Since O'Neill had never been able to compose at a typewriter or by dictation, his writing career, apart from some revisions, was effectively over. Furthermore, he was extremely depressed by the Second World War: it made his writing seem of little consequence and the staging of his work even less important and appropriate. Consequently, he refused to authorise productions of new plays; none appeared between *Days Without End* in 1933 and *The Iceman*

Cometh in 1946. When the latter was finally staged, the inadequate production did little to restore interest in O'Neill's work.

Throughout his life, O'Neill had roamed far in search of a home and a sense of belonging: New York, Connecticut, Provincetown, Bermuda, France, Georgia, California. Sometime before his death on 27 November 1953, O'Neill struggled up from his bed to complain 'I knew it, I knew it! Born in a goddam hotel room and dying in a hotel room!' Only with the posthumous revival of *The Iceman Cometh* and the first production of *Long Day's Journey into Night* in 1956 did his reputation, like his life, come full circle.

Christine Dymkowski
Lecturer in Drama and Theatre Studies
Royal Holloway and Bedford New College
University of London

Introduction to the Play

By June 1939, O'Neill had spent four and a half years at work on his ambitious play-cycle, *A Tale of Possessors, Self-Dispossessed*, and was becoming 'fed up and stale' with it. Laying it aside, he read over old notes containing ideas for single plays and decided to work on the two that 'appeal most . . . the Jimmy the P[riest's] H[ell] H[ole] Garden idea and N[ew] L[ondon] family one' (Work Diary, 5 & 6 June, quoted in Floyd, p. 260). This fresh start resulted in the two plays that O'Neill considered his best, *The Iceman Cometh* and *Long Day's Journey into Night*.

The gestation of the two plays was both quick and closely intertwined: within a month, O'Neill had outlined both of them, the scenario for *The Iceman Cometh* being written between 9–24 June and that for *Long Day's Journey* between 25 June–3 July. O'Neill returned to *Iceman* on 6 July, finishing the first draft on 12 October, the second on 26 November, and the third on 14 December; by 3 January 1940 he had completed the final correcting, cutting, and 'trimming' (Work Diary, quoted in Floyd, p. 276). That he was able to move so smoothly from one play to the other is not surprising: both are heavily autobiographical, and both are set in the playwright's watershed year of 1912.

The action of *The Iceman Cometh* takes place in Harry Hope's bar, an amalgam of the watering-holes the youthful O'Neill had frequented in New York: Jimmy-the-Priest's on the waterfront, the Hell Hole in Greenwich Village, and the bar of the Garden Hotel on Madison Avenue. The denizens of Harry Hope's include people O'Neill knew well, those he only knew about, and partial self-portraits. Identifying their real-life counterparts does not call for much critical conjecture, since O'Neill's early character sketches actually name the friends and acquaintances who appear in the play. Hugo Kalmar was Hippolyte Havel, a Czechoslovak revolutionary, one-time lover of Emma Goldman, and eventual partner of O'Neill's Greenwich Village friend Polly Holladay; his physical description and speech habits are accurately duplicated in O'Neill's play. Harry Hope was modelled on Tom Wallace, proprietor of the Hell Hole and virtual recluse, and Joe Mott on O'Neill's gambler friend Joe Smith. Ed Mosher

was a combination of two circus workers O'Neill had known, Bill
Clarke and Jack Croak, while Captain Lewis was a 'same as life'
portrait of Major Adams (O'Neill's first list of characters, quoted
in Floyd, p. 261). Even the two bartenders, Rocky and Chuck,
had actual counterparts; only the three women (Pearl, Margie,
Cora) and three policemen (McGloin, Moran, Lieb) are
generic portraits.

The models for Larry Slade and James Cameron were both
very important in O'Neill's life. The former is a portrait of Terry
Carlin, one-time anarchist, Nietzschean enthusiast, and dedicated
alcoholic, who was in many ways O'Neill's mentor, influencing his
thinking and reading. O'Neill had met him around 1915 and
remained in touch for the rest of Carlin's life, helping to support
him and even paying his funeral expenses in 1934. James
Findlater Byth, whom O'Neill had already commemorated in an
early story called 'Tomorrow' and an early one-act play called
Exorcism, reappears in *Iceman* as James Cameron, or 'Jimmy
Tomorrow'. He had been a press agent for O'Neill's father and
boasted that he had been a Reuters correspondent during the
Boer War, a claim O'Neill evidently believed; in fact, he had done
publicity work for a Boer War theatrical spectacle and passed on
to O'Neill much of the historical fact that informs Lewis's and
Wetjoen's reminiscences in *Iceman* (these names are also drawn
from his stories). Byth had been a fellow-roomer at Jimmy-the-
Priest's when O'Neill attempted suicide in 1912; it was Byth who
broke into O'Neill's room and rescued him from the Veronal
overdose he had taken. The following year, still living at Jimmy-
the-Priest's, Byth committed suicide himself by leaping from a
window, a death given to Parritt in *Iceman*.

Other characters originate from newspaper stories. Willie
Oban, for example, is modelled on a son of Al Adams, a
renowned criminal who had been involved in fraudulent policy
and brokerage dealings. Parritt seems to have been based on
Donald Vose, whose mother was an anarchist and friend of
Emma Goldman; he had betrayed the bombers responsible for
dynamiting the *Los Angeles Times* building in 1910. Those
betrayed did not include his mother: the motivating force for
Parritt's treachery, love-hate for his mother, rather reflects
O'Neill's own feelings. Interestingly, Carlin had talked to O'Neill
about the Vose case, and this link reveals a possible further
connection between Slade/Carlin and Parritt/Vose in O'Neill's
mind: Carlin may have supplied his and O'Neill's mutual friend
Louis Holladay with heroin for a successful suicide attempt,
mirroring Slade's sanction of Parritt's self-punishment.

Hickey's genesis is more complex than that of the other characters. In a letter to the critic George Jean Nathan, O'Neill explained that he had known 'a periodical drunk salesman, . . . a damned amusing likable guy', who made jokes about his wife and the iceman and sometimes 'boozily harped on the slogan that honesty is the best policy' (8 February 1940, quoted in *Selected Letters*, p. 501). However, he wrote to Kenneth Macgowan in a completely different vein that he 'never knew [Hickey]. He's the most imaginary character in the play. . . . He is all of [the periodical drunk salesmen I knew], you might say, and none of them' (30 December 1940, quoted in *'The Theatre We Worked For'*, p. 258). Arthur and Barbara Gelb have commented on Hickey's resemblance to a Hell Hole regular called Happy, who was a collector for a laundry chain, and to O'Neill's brother Jamie (*O'Neill*, p. 285); Barlow supports the latter contention, commenting that Jamie had not only been a travelling salesman but had also played one in a popular comedy (*Final Acts*, p. 14). Sheaffer makes a convincing case for similarities to the famous Charles E. Chapin murder case of 1918; Chapin had 'shot his wife in the head as she slept and insisted afterward that he had been motivated by love, by concern for her welfare' (*Son & Artist*, p. 494). And, of course, in his ambivalence towards his wife Evelyn, Hickey notably resembles his creator's own contradictory feelings towards women, particularly towards his wife and his mother. He also voices the common O'Neill complaint that only punishment by others can drive out self-punishment: 'There's a limit to the guilt you can feel and the forgiveness and the pity you can take!' (Act IV).

Hickey's origins are especially interesting because, although the catalyst of the play's action, he did not necessarily figure in O'Neill's original conception of *Iceman*. Floyd argues that Hickey was an afterthought: he is absent from the original list of characters, many of his characteristics are originally assigned to the bartender called Bull, and he is first mentioned at the end of the Act One outline (*O'Neill at Work*, pp. 267–68). The reason for this seemingly reticent introduction of Hickey into the play may lie in his uncomfortable resemblance to O'Neill himself. Sheaffer points out obvious parallels between them: not only did both enjoy periodical drunken binges, but the playwright inherited his theatrical flair from his father just as Hickey derived his persuasive patter from his preacher father. He also highlights a more subtle similarity: O'Neill stopped drinking in 1926 towards the end of psychoanalytical work that revealed to him his negative feelings about his mother, just as Hickey gives up alcohol after killing his wife. Nearly all of O'Neill's other self-portraits reflect his own appearance and personality, but stage directions specify that Hickey is 'a little under medium height, with a stout, roly-poly figure', round face, and bald head (Act I), the exact opposite of O'Neill. As Sheaffer reflects, the playwright, 'burning to voice through Hickey some of his darkest impulses, took pains to mislead anyone trying to follow his biographical tracks in his writings' (Son & Artist, pp. 501–2).

The Iceman Cometh also shows the influence of O'Neill's reading. Its parallels with Ibsen's The Wild Duck, in which Gregers Werle destroys not only the 'life-lie' but the lives that are dependent on it, are as obvious as its differences. Several commentators have also pointed out resemblances to Gorky's The Lower Depths, a play O'Neill admired, and Barlow discusses similarities to William Saroyan's The Time of Your Life, though it is by no means certain that O'Neill knew the play when he wrote his own (Final Acts, pp. 16–17).

Critics have also emphasized the links between Iceman and O'Neill's earlier works, such as Lazarus Laughed and Anna Christie (see Final Acts, pp. 17 and 168n, for discussion of this criticism). O'Neill clearly had his earlier story about James Byth in mind as he wrote and in fact thought of calling the play Tomorrow or Credit Tomorrow (Final Acts, p. 17). The title he finally chose resonates on many levels. O'Neill told his friend Dudley Nichols that the iceman is death, but the title also alludes to the old joke about a husband calling to his wife 'Has the iceman come yet?' and receiving the reply 'No, but he's breathing hard'. Here, the iceman is the proverbial figure, like the milkman or mailman, whose daily visit to the home brings news, sexual interest, and a whiff of the outside world. The title further alludes to Christ's arrival in Matthew 25:6, which O'Neill knew well and which, as Sheaffer points out, had also inspired the title of Waldo Frank's novel The Bridegroom Cometh (Son & Artist, p. 484).

Although O'Neill had finished writing the play in 1940, he did not want it produced until the war had been over for about a year: he felt its negative spirit, out of step with the exhilaration of peace, would echo the disenchantment sure to follow. The Theatre Guild, which during the war had negotiated with O'Neill to produce A Moon for the Misbegotten, The Iceman Cometh, A Touch of the Poet, and Hughie when the time was ripe, consequently made plans to open their 1946 season with Iceman, the first O'Neill play to be seen in New York since Days without End had closed in 1934. It also proved to be the last new O'Neill play seen there during the playwright's lifetime: the Guild never produced either *Poet* or *Hughie*, and *Moon* closed during its pre-Broadway try-out.

The production, which opened on 9 October at the Martin Beck Theatre, was directed by Eddie Dowling (who was originally meant to play Hickey as well as to direct) and featured James Barton as Hickey, Carl Benton Reid as Slade, Paul Crabtree as Parritt, and Dudley Digges as Hope. The play opened at 4.30 p.m. and finished at 10.00 p.m., with a 75-minute dinner break after Act I from 5.30–6.45 p.m.; later, because some of the audience failed to return for the rest of the play, the dinner break was omitted and the play performed from 7.30 p.m. to 11.20 p.m., 15 minutes of playing-time being cut by virtue of a quicker pace. *Iceman* as performed was in fact considerably shorter than the published text which appeared simultaneously with the production: besides pruning the play in 1945 for production and publication, O'Neill cut a further 4000 words before rehearsal began and another 2500 words during rehearsal (see Barlow, *Final Acts*, pp. 21–23, 56, 60 and Vena, *O'Neill's 'The Iceman Cometh'*, pp. 44–45 and Appendix A, for details of these considerable cuts). He dug in his heels when necessary, however: when Lawrence Langner, one of the Guild's directors, complained that the same idea had been expressed eighteen times, O'Neill replied that he '*intended* it to be repeated eighteen times!' (quoted in Sheaffer, *Son & Artist*, p. 572).

The Theatre Guild production, which ran for 136 performances, had a mixed reception. The acting and direction were generally praised, but the play itself drew a more divided response. There were universal complaints about its length and repetition; even the many critics who admired the play felt that it could have been improved by pruning. Others felt the faults were more basic: Howard Barnes, for example, judged the play 'essentially earthbound and monotonous' despite its 'fascinating characters', 'reverent . . . production', and 'generally inspired acting' (*NY Herald Tribune*, 10 October 1946).

Not until *Iceman* was revived by José Quintero ten years later, on 8 May 1956, did the play come into its own, prompting a revival of interest in the by-then neglected dramatist. Brooks Atkinson, whose admiring review of the original production nevertheless complained that the characters 'talk too much', found that in Quintero's uncut production 'every part of [a long script came] alive' (*NY Times*, 10 October 1946 and 9 May 1956; the quotations following are also from his 1956 review). Performed at the Circle in the Square, a former nightclub that had been converted into an intimate theatre with an arena stage,

this production gave the audience a 'sensation of participating.
The rows of seats are only an extension of . . . the battered,
blowzy waterfront saloon . . .'. Another advantage was the
tremendous performance of Jason Robards Jr., who played
Hickey 'like an evangelist', an element missing from the first
production (along with lines that explained Hickey's background
as a preacher's son). The production achieved a magnificent run
of 565 performances and launched both Quintero and Robards
as O'Neill's most successful exponents: six months later, at
Carlotta Monterey's invitation, the two joined forces again for the
first American production of *Long Day's Journey into Night*.

Some of the reviewers of the 1956 production commented on
the play's resemblance to Beckett's *Waiting for Godot*, first
performed in 1953. The shift in theatrical taste that had occurred
between *Iceman*'s premiere and its 1956 revival is also noted in
some of the reviews of the first London production, which
opened on 29 January 1958 at the Arts Theatre club: one
reviewer supposes that the play's original cool reception was due
to 'despair ['s being] not nearly so fashionable as it has since
become' (Milton Shulman, *Evening Standard*, 30 January 1958).
Peter Wood's production of the uncut text, which featured Ian
Bannen as Hickey and Patrick Magee as Slade, was by all
accounts superb: it was the greatest success the Arts had had, the
originally scheduled run being extended for a month. The
production transferred on 29 March to the much larger Winter
Garden, closing on 10 May. Although critics were virtually
unanimous in judging that *Iceman* could profitably be cut by at
least an hour, they were similarly agreed that the length did not
damage a rich theatrical experience. Many reviewers noted the
production's rewarding exploitation of the play's humour, an
aspect of O'Neill's writing that generally seems to have been
better appreciated in this country than in the playwright's own.

Both the Royal Shakespeare Company and the National
Theatre have staged *The Iceman Cometh*; the former opened at the
Aldwych on 18 June 1976 in a production by Howard Davies and
the latter at the Cottesloe on 4 March 1980 in a production by
Bill Bryden. On both occasions, critical reception of the play itself
was mixed, though on the whole reviewers preferred the RSC
production, which seems to have retained more of the play's
initial humour than the subsequent revival did. The National
production was further hampered by a setting that arranged the
characters in a two-dimensional frieze, thus ensuring the static
movement on which O'Neill himself had insisted during
rehearsals for the Theatre Guild production. However, as Irving

Wardle and many other critics pointed out, the 'scenic monotony . . . intensifie[d] the repetitiousness of the text' (*The Times*, 6 March 1980). Interestingly, despite the playwright's stage directions, Jack Shepherd, who played Hickey in this production, was made up to look like O'Neill himself.

In his review of the 1958 London production, Kenneth Tynan had sought to answer why the play held him despite its manifest faults. He decided that it was because of 'the insight it gives us into O'Neill himself. It is a dramatised neurosis, with no holds barred, written in a vein of unsparing, implacable honesty' (*Observer*, 2 February 1958). O'Neill, in a 1944 letter to Lawrence Langner about his experiments with a tape-recorder now that writing had become so physically difficult, seems to agree:

> a couple of days ago . . . I read into the mike of the Sound Scriber a favorite bit of mine from *The Iceman Cometh* – Act Three, the brief passage between Hickey and Larry when Larry is forced to admit, while refusing to admit, that his saving dream that he is finished with life and sick of it and will welcome the long sleep of death is just a pipe dream. When I played the record back and listened to the voice that was my voice and yet not my voice saying: 'I'm afraid to live, am I? – and even more afraid to die! . . .' – well, it sure did something to me. It wasn't Larry, it was my ghost talking to me, or I to my ghost. . . . It really was quite a moment of strange drama. (13 May 1944, quoted in *Selected Letters*, pp. 556–57.)

In *The Iceman Cometh*, O'Neill once again lays bare the 'strange drama' of his self-tormenting soul.

Christine Dymkowski
February 1992

Sources

Barlow, Judith. *Final Acts: The Creation of Three Late O'Neill Plays*. Athens: The University of Georgia Press, 1985.

Bogard, Travis and Jackson R. Breyer, eds. *Selected Letters of Eugene O'Neill*. New Haven & London: Yale University Press, 1988.

Bryer, Jackson R., ed. *'The Theatre We Worked For': The Letters of Eugene O'Neill to Kenneth Macgowan*. New Haven and London: Yale University Press, 1982.

Cargill, Oscar, et al., eds. *O'Neill and His Plays: Four Decades of Criticism*. New York: New York University Press, 1961.

Floyd, Virginia, ed. *Eugene O'Neill at Work: Newly Released Ideas for Plays*. New York: Frederick Ungar, 1981.

Gelb, Arthur and Barbara. *O'Neill*. New York: Harper, 1960.

Miller, Jordan Y. *Eugene O'Neill and the American Critic: A Summary and Bibliographical Checklist*. Second edition, revised. Hamden, Connecticut: Archon, 1973.

Ranald, Margaret Loftus. *The Eugene O'Neill Companion*. Westport, Conn., and London: Greenwood, 1984.

Sheaffer, Louis. *O'Neill: Son & Playwright*. London: Dent, 1968.
————————. *O'Neill: Son & Artist*. London: Paul Elek, 1973.

Vena, Gary. *O'Neill's 'The Iceman Cometh': Reconstructing the Premiere*. Ann Arbor: UMI Research Press, 1988.

I would also like to thank Sue Cusworth of RHBNC for help both in tracing British productions of O'Neill's plays and in obtaining copies of reviews.

List of O'Neill's Produced Plays

Title	Year Written*	First Production	First London Production
The Web	1913–14	39th Street Theatre, New York 17 March 1924	
Thirst	1913–14	Wharf Theatre, Provincetown, Mass. Summer 1916	
Fog	1913–14	Playwrights' Theater, New York 5 January 1917	
Bound East for Cardiff	1913–14	Wharf Theatre, Provincetown, Mass. 28 July 1916	(see *S.S. Glencairn*)
Servitude	1913–14	Skylark Theatre N.Y. International Airport 22 April 1960	
Abortion	1913–14	Key Theatre, New York 27 October 1959	
The Movie Man	1914	Key Theatre, New York 27 October 1959	

The Sniper	1915	Playwright's Theater, New York 16 February 1917	
Before Breakfast	1916	Playwrights' Theater, New York 1 December 1916	Gate Theatre 30 August 1926
Ile	1916–17	Playwrights' Theater, New York 30 November 1917	Everyman Theatre 17 April 1922
In the Zone	1916–17	Comedy Theater, New York (Washington Square Players) 31 October 1917	Everyman Theatre 15 June 1921
The Long Voyage Home	1916–17	Playwrights' Theater, New York 2 November 1917	Everyman Theatre 12 June 1925
The Moon of The Caribbees	1916–17	Playwrights' Theater, New York 20 December 1918	(see *S.S. Glencairn*)
S.S. Glencairn (*Bound East for Cardiff, In the Zone, Moon of the Caribbees,* and *Long Voyage Home*)		Barnstormer's Barn Provincetown, Massachusetts 14 August 1924	Mercury Theatre 9 June 1947
The Rope	1918	Playwrights' Theater, New York 26 April 1918	

Title	Year Written*	First Production	First London Production
The Dreamy Kid	1918	Playwrights' Theater, New York 31 October 1919	(Festival Theatre, Cambridge 14 May 1928)
Beyond the Horizon	1918	Morosco Theater, New York 3 February 1920	Regent Theatre (The Repertory Players) 31 January 1926
Where the Cross is Made	1918	Playwrights' Theater, New York 22 November 1918	Arts Theatre 27 October 1927
The Straw	1918–19	Greenwich Village Theater, New York 10 November 1921 (after an out-of-town try-out)	
Exorcism	1919	Playwrights' Theater, New York 26 March 1920	
Chris (1st version of *Anna Christie*)	1919	Apollo Theater, Atlantic City, N.J. 8 March 1920	
Gold	1920	Frazee Theater, New York 1 June 1921	

Anna Christie	1920	Vanderbilt Theater, New York 2 November 1921	Strand Theatre 10 April 1923
The Emperor Jones	1920	Playwrights' Theater, New York 1 November 1920	Ambassadors' Theatre 10 September 1925
Diff'rent	1920	Playwrights' Theater, New York 27 December 1920	Everyman Theatre 4 October 1921
The First Man	1921	Neighborhood Playhouse, New York 4 March 1922	
The Hairy Ape	1921	Playwrights' Theater, New York 9 March 1922	Gate Theatre 26 January 1928
The Fountain	1921–22	Greenwich Village Theater. New York 10 December 1925	
Welded	1922–23	39th Street Theater, New York 17 March 1924	The Playroom Six 16 February 1928
All God's Chillun Got Wings	1923	Provincetown Playhouse, New York 15 May 1924	Gate Theatre 8 November 1926
The Ancient Mariner (adaptation)	1924	Provincetown Playhouse (previously Playwrights' Theater), New York 6 April 1924	

Title	Year Written*	First Production	First London Production
Desire Under The Elms	1924	Greenwich Village Theater, New York 11 November 1924	Gate Theatre 24 February 1931
Marco Millions	1923–25	Guild Theater, New York 9 January 1928	Westminster Theatre 26 December 1938 (also produced at Festival Theatre, Cambridge, 1932)
The Great God Brown	1925	Greenwich Village Theater, New York 23 January 1926	Strand Theatre (Stage Society) 19 June 1927
Lazarus Laughed	1925–26	Pasadena Community Playhouse, California 9 April 1928	
Strange Interlude	1926–27	John Golden Theater, New York 30 January 1928	Lyric Theatre 3 February 1931
Dynamo	1928	Martin Beck Theater, New York 11 February 1929	
Mourning Becomes Electra	1929–31	Guild Theater, New York 26 October 1931	Westminster Theatre 19 November 1937

Play	Date		
Ah! Wilderness	1932	Nixon Theater, Pittsburgh, Pennsylvania 25 September 1933 (out-of-town tryout before New York opening at Guild Theater, 2 October 1933)	Westminster Theatre 4 May 1936
Days Without End	1932–33	Plymouth Theater, Boston, Mass. 27 December 1933 (out-of-town tryout before New York opening at Guild Theater, 8 January 1934)	Grafton Theatre (Stage Society) 3 February 1935
A Touch of the Poet	1935–42	Royal Dramatic Theatre, Stockholm, Sweden 29 March 1957 (first American production at Helen Hayes Theater, New York, 2 October 1958)	Young Vic Theatre 20 January 1988 (also produced at Ashcroft Theatre, Croydon, 16 September 1963)
More Stately Mansions	1936–42	Royal Dramatic Theatre, Stockholm, Sweden 11 September 1962 (first American production at Ahmanson Theater, Los Angeles, California, 12 November 1967)	Greenwich Theatre 19 September 1974
The Iceman Cometh	1939	Martin Beck Theater, New York 9 October 1946	Arts Theatre 29 January 1958

Title	Year Written*	First Production	First London Production
Long Day's Journey into Night	1939–41	Royal Dramatic Theatre. Stockholm, Sweden 10 February 1956 (first American production at Helen Hayes Theater, New York, 7 November 1956)	Globe Theatre 24 September 1958 (transfer from Lyceum Theatre, Edinburgh, 8 September 1958)
Hughie	1941–42	Royal Dramatic Theatre, Stockholm, Sweden 18 September 1958	Duchess Theatre 18 June 1963
A Moon for the Misbegotten	1943	Hartman Theater, Columbus, Ohio (Guild Theater production) 20 February 1947	Arts Theatre 20 January 1960

*Dates of composition are approximate.

THE ICEMAN COMETH

Characters

HARRY HOPE, proprietor of a saloon and rooming house*
ED MOSHER, HOPE's brother-in-law, one-time circus man*
PAT MCGLOIN, one-time Police Lieutenant*
WILLIE OBAN, a Harvard Law School alumnus*
JOE MOTT, one-time proprietor of a Negro gambling house
PIET WETJOEN ('THE GENERAL'), one-time leader of a Boer commando*
CECIL LEWIS ('THE CAPTAIN'), one-time Captain of British infantry*
JAMES CAMERON ('JIMMY TOMORROW'), one-time Boer War correspondent*
HUGO KALMAR, one-time editor of Anarchist periodicals
LARRY SLADE, one-time Syndicalist-Anarchist*
ROCKY PIOGGI, night bartender*
DON PARRITT*
PEARL* ⎫
MARGIE* ⎬ street-walkers
CORA ⎭
CHUCK MORELLO, day bartender*
THEODORE HICKMAN (HICKEY), a hardware salesman
MORAN
LIEB

*Roomers at Harry Hope's

Scenes

ACT ONE

Back room and a section of the bar at Harry Hope's. Early morning in summer, 1912.

ACT TWO

Back room, around midnight of the same day.

ACT THREE

Bar and a section of the back room. Morning of the following day.

ACT FOUR

Same as Act One. Back room and a section of the bar. Around 1.30 a.m. of the next day.

General Scene

Harry Hope's is a Raines-Law hotel of the period, a cheap ginmill of the five-cent whisky, last-resort variety situated on the downtown West Side of New York. The building, owned by Hope, is a narrow five-storey structure of the tenement type, the second floor a flat occupied by the proprietor. The renting of rooms on the upper floors, under the Raines-Law loopholes, makes the establishment legally a hotel and gives it the privilege of serving liquor in the back room of the bar after closing hours and on Sundays, provided a meal is served with the booze, thus making a back room legally a hotel restaurant. This food provision was generally circumvented by putting a property sandwich in the middle of each table, an old desiccated ruin of dust-laden bread and mummified ham or cheese which only the drunkest yokel from the sticks ever regarded as anything but a noisome table decoration. But at Harry Hope's, Hope being a former minor Tammanyite and still possessing friends, this food technicality is ignored as irrelevant, except during the fleeting alarms of reform agitation. Even Hope's back room is not a separate room, but simply the rear of the bar-room divided from the bar by drawing a dirty black curtain across the room.

ACT ONE

Scene. The back room and a section of the bar of HARRY HOPE's
saloon on an early morning in summer, 1912.

*The right wall of the back room is a dirty black curtain which separates it
from the bar. At rear, this curtain is drawn back from the wall so the
bartender can get in and out. The back room is crammed with round
tables and chairs placed so close together that it is a difficult squeeze to
pass between them. In the middle of the rear wall is a door opening on a
hallway. In the left corner, built out into the room, is the toilet with a sign
'This is it' on the door. Against the middle of the left wall is a nickel-in-
the-slot phonograph. Two windows, so glazed with grime one cannot see
through them, are in the left wall, looking out on a backyard. The walls
and ceiling once were white, but it was a long time ago, and they are now
so splotched, peeled, stained and dusty that their colour can best be
described as dirty. The floor, with iron spittoons placed here and there, is
covered with sawdust. Lighting comes from single wall-brackets, two at
left and two at rear.*

*There are three rows of tables, from front to back. Three are in the front
line. The one at left-front has four chairs; the one at centre-front, four;
the one at right-front, five. At rear of, and half between, front tables one
and two is a table of the second row with five chairs. A table, similarly
placed at rear of front tables two and three, also has five chairs. The
third row of tables, four chairs to one and six to the other, is against the
rear wall on either side of the door.*

*At right of this dividing curtain is a section of the bar-room, with the end
of the bar seen at rear, a door to the hall at left of it. At front is a table
with four chairs. Light comes from the street windows off right, the grey
subdued light of early morning in a narrow street. In the back room,*
LARRY SLADE *and* HUGO KALMAR *are at the table at left-front,*
HUGO *in a chair facing right,* LARRY *at rear of table facing front,
with an empty chair between them. A fourth chair is at right of table,
facing left.* HUGO *is a small man in his late fifties. He has a head
much too big for his body, a high forehead, crinkly long black hair
streaked with grey, a square face with a pug nose, a walrus moustache,
black eyes which peer near-sightedly from behind thick-lensed spectacles,
tiny hands and feet. He is dressed in threadbare black clothes and his
white shirt is frayed at collar and cuffs, but everything about him is*

fastidiously clean. Even his flowing tie is neatly tied. There is a foreign atmosphere about him, the stamp of an alien radical, a strong resemblance to the type Anarchist as portrayed, bomb in hand, in newspaper cartoons. He is asleep now, bent forward in his chair, his arms folded on the table, his head resting sideways on his arms.

LARRY SLADE *is sixty. He is tall, raw-boned, with coarse straight white hair, worn long and raggedly cut. He has a gaunt Irish face with a big nose, high cheek-bones, a lantern jaw with a week's stubble of beard, a mystic's meditative pale-blue eyes with a gleam of sharp sardonic humour in them. As slovenly as* HUGO *is neat, his clothes are dirty and much slept in. His grey flannel shirt, open at the neck, has the appearance of having never been washed. From the way he methodically scratches himself with his long-fingered, hairy hands, he is lousy and reconciled to being so. He is the only occupant of the room who is not asleep. He stares in front of him, an expression of tired tolerance giving his face the quality of a pitying but weary old priest's.*

All four chairs at the middle table, front, are occupied. JOE MOTT *sits at left-front of the table, facing front. Behind him, facing right-front, is* PIET WETJOEN *('The General'). At centre of the table, rear,* JAMES CAMERON *('Jimmy Tomorrow') sits facing front. At right of table, opposite* JOE, *is* CECIL LEWIS *('The Captain').*

JOE MOTT *is a Negro, about fifty years old, brown-skinned, stocky, wearing a light suit that had once been flashily sporty but is now about to fall apart. His pointed tan buttoned shoes, faded pink shirt and bright tie belong to the same vintage. Still, he manages to preserve an atmosphere of nattiness and there is nothing dirty about his appearance. His face is only mildly negroid in type. The nose is thin and his lips are not noticeably thick. His hair is crinkly and he is beginning to get bald. A scar from a knife slash runs from his left cheek-bone to jaw. His face would be hard and tough if it were not for its good nature and lazy humour. He is asleep, his nodding head supported by his left hand.*

PIET WETJOEN, *the Boer, is in his fifties, a huge man wit.: a bald head and a long grizzled beard. He is slovenly dressed in a dirty shapeless patched suit, spotted by food. A Dutch farmer type, his once great muscular strength has been debauched into flaccid tallow. But despite his blubbery mouth and sodden bloodshot blue eyes, there is still a suggestion of old authority lurking in him like a memory of the drowned. He is hunched forward, both elbows on the table, his hand on each side of his head for support.*

JAMES CAMERON *('Jimmy Tomorrow') is about the same size and age as* HUGO, *a small man. Like* HUGO *he wears threadbare black, and everything about him is clean. But the resemblance ceases there.* JIMMY *has a face like an old well-bred gentle bloodhound's, with folds of flesh hanging from each side of his mouth, and big brown friendly guileless eyes, more bloodshot than any bloodhound's ever were. He has mouse-coloured thinning hair, a little bulbous nose, buck teeth in a small rabbit mouth. But his forehead is fine, his eyes are intelligent and there once was a competent ability in him. His speech is educated, with the ghost of a Scotch rhythm in it. His manners are those of a gentleman. There is a quality about him of a prim, Victorian old maid, and at the same time of a likeable affectionate boy who has never grown up. He sleeps, chin on chest, hands folded in his lap.*

CECIL LEWIS *('The Captain') is as obviously English as Yorkshire pudding and just as obviously the former army officer. He is going on sixty. His hair and military moustache are white, his eyes bright blue, his complexion that of a turkey. His lean figure is still erect and square-shouldered. He is stripped to the waist, his coat, shirt, undershirt, collar and tie crushed up into a pillow on the table in front of him, his head sideways on this pillow, facing front, his arms dangling towards the floor. On his lower left shoulder is the big ragged scar of an old wound.*

At the table at right, HARRY HOPE, *the proprietor, sits in the middle, facing front, with* PAT MCGLOIN *on his right and* ED MOSHER *on his left, the other two chairs being unoccupied.*

Both MCGLOIN *and* MOSHER *are big paunchy men.* MCGLOIN *has his old occupation of policeman stamped all over him. He is in his fifties, sandy-haired, bullet-headed, jowly, with protruding ears and little round eyes. His face must once have been brutal and greedy, but time and whisky have melted it down into a good-humoured, parasite's characterlessness. He wears old clothes and is slovenly. He is slumped sideways on his chair, his head drooping jerkily towards one shoulder.*

ED MOSHER *is going on sixty. He has a round kewpie's face – a kewpie who is an unshaven habitual drunkard. He looks like an enlarged, elderly, bald edition of the village fat boy – a sly fat boy, congenitally indolent, a practical joker, a born grafter and con merchant. But amusing and essentially harmless, even in his most enterprising days, because always too lazy to carry crookedness beyond petty swindling. The influence of his old circus career is apparent in his get-up. His worn clothes are flashy; he wears phony rings and a heavy brass watch-chain (not connected to a watch). Like* MCGLOIN, *he is slovenly. His head is thrown back, his big mouth open.*

HARRY HOPE *is sixty, white-haired, so thin the description 'bag of bones' was made for him. He has the face of an old family horse, prone to tantrums, with balkiness always smouldering in its wall eyes, waiting for any excuse to shy and pretend to take the bit in its teeth.* HOPE *is one of those men whom everyone likes on sight, a soft-hearted slob, without malice, feeling superior to no one, a sinner among sinners, a born easy mark for every appeal. He attempts to hide his defencelessness behind a testy truculent manner, but this has never fooled anyone. He is a little deaf, but not half as deaf as he sometimes pretends. His sight is failing but is not as bad as he complains it is. He wears five-and-ten-cent-store spectacles which are so out of alignment that one eye at times peers half over one glass while the other eye looks half under the other. He has badly fitting store teeth, which click like castanets when he begins to fume. He is dressed in an old coat from one suit and pants from another.*

In a chair facing right at the table in the second line, between the first two tables, front, sits WILLIE OBAN, *his head on his left arm outstretched along the table edge. He is in his late thirties, of average height, thin. His haggard, dissipated face has a small nose, a pointed chin, blue eyes with colourless lashes and brows. His blond hair, badly in need of a cut, clings in a limp part to his skull. His eyelids flutter continually as if any light were too strong for his eyes. The clothes he wears belong on a scarecrow. They seem constructed of an inferior grade of dirty blotting paper. His shoes are even more disreputable, wrecks of imitation leather, one laced with twine, the other with a bit of wire. He has no socks, and his bare feet show through holes in the soles, with his big toes sticking out of the uppers. He keeps muttering and twitching in his sleep.*

As the curtain rises, ROCKY, *the night bartender, comes from the bar through the curtain and stands looking over the back room. He is a Neapolitan-American in his late twenties, squat and muscular, with a flat, swarthy face and beady eyes. The sleeves of his collarless shirt are rolled up on his thick, powerful arms and he wears a soiled apron. A tough guy but sentimental, in his way, and good-natured. He signals to* LARRY *with a cautious 'Sstt' and motions him to see if* HOPE *is asleep.* LARRY *rises from his chair to look at* HOPE *and nods to* ROCKY. ROCKY *goes back in the bar but immediately returns with a bottle of bar whisky and a glass. He squeezes between the tables to* LARRY.

ROCKY (*in a low voice out of the side of his mouth*). Make it fast.

LARRY *pours a drink and gulps it down.* ROCKY *takes the bottle and puts it on the table where* WILLIE OBAN *is.*

Don't want de Boss to get wise when he's got one of his tightwad buns on. (*He chuckles with an amused glance at* HOPE.) Jees, ain't de old bastard a riot when he starts dat bull about turnin' over a new leaf? 'Not a damned drink on de house,' he tells me, 'and all dese bums got to pay up deir room rent.

Beginnin' tomorrow,' he says. Jees, yuh'd tink he meant it! (*He sits down in the chair at* LARRY's *left*.)

LARRY (*grinning*). I'll be glad to pay up – tomorrow. And I know my fellow inmates will promise the same. They've all a touching credulity concerning tomorrows. (*A half-drunken mockery in his eyes*.) It'll be a great day for them, tomorrow – the Feast of All Fools, with brass bands playing! Their ships will come in, loaded to the gunwales with cancelled regrets and promises fulfilled and clean slates and new leases!

ROCKY (*cynically*). Yeah, and a ton of Hop!

LARRY (*leans toward him, a comical intensity in his low voice*). Don't mock the faith! Have you no respect for religion, you unregenerate Wop? What's it matter if the truth is that their favouring breeze has the stink of nickel whisky on its breath, and their sea is a growler of lager and ale, and their ships are long since looted and scuttled and sunk on the bottom? To hell with the truth! As the history of the world proves, the truth has no bearing on anything. It's irrelevant and immaterial, as the lawyers say. The lie of a pipe dream is what gives life to the whole misbegotten mad lot of us, drunk or sober. And that's enough philosophic wisdom to give you for one drink of rot-gut.

ROCKY (*grins kiddingly*). De old Foolosopher, like Hickey calls yuh, ain't yuh? I s'pose you don't fall for no pipe dream?

LARRY (*a bit stiffly*). I don't, no. Mine are all dead and buried behind me. What's before me is the comforting fact that death is a fine long sleep, and I'm damned tired, and it can't come too soon for me.

ROCKY. Yeah, just hangin' around hopin' you'll croak, ain't yuh? Well, I'm bettin' you'll have a good long wait. Jees, somebody'll have to take an axe to croak you!

LARRY (*grins*). Yes, it's my bad luck to be cursed with an iron constitution that even Harry's booze can't corrode.

ROCKY. De old anarchist wise guy dat knows all de answers! Dat's you, huh?

LARRY (*frowns*). Forget the anarchist part of it. I'm through with the Movement long since. I saw men didn't want to be saved from themselves, for that would mean they'd have to give up greed, and they'll never pay that price for liberty. So I said to the world, God bless all here, and may the best man win and die of gluttony! And I took a seat in the grandstand of philosophical detachment to fall asleep observing the cannibals do their death dance. (*He chuckles at his own fancy – reaches over and shakes* HUGO's *shoulder.*) Ain't I telling him the truth, Comrade Hugo?

ROCKY. Aw, fer Chris' sake, don't get dat bughouse bum started!

HUGO (*raises his head and peers at* ROCKY *blearily through his thick spectacles – in a guttural declamatory tone*). Capitalist swine! Bourgeois stool pigeons! Have the slaves no right to sleep even? (*Then he grins at* ROCKY *and his manner changes to a giggling, wheedling playfulness, as though he were talking to a child.*) Hello, leedle Rocky! Leedle monkey-face! Vere is your leedle slave-girls? (*With an abrupt change to a bullying tone.*) Don't be a fool! Loan me a dollar! Damned bourgeois Wop! The great Malatesta is my good friend! Buy me a trink! (*He seems to run down, and is overcome by drowsiness. His head sinks to the table again and he is at once fast asleep.*)

ROCKY. He's out again. (*More exasperated than angry.*) He's lucky no one don't take his cracks serious or he'd wake up every mornin' in hospital.

LARRY (*regarding* HUGO *with pity*). No. No one takes him seriously. That's his epitaph. Not even the comrades any more. If I've been through with the Movement long since, it's been through with him, and, thanks to whisky, he's the only one doesn't know it.

ROCKY. I've let him get by wid too much. He's goin' to pull dat slave-girl stuff on me once too often. (*His manner changes to defensive argument.*) Hell, yuh'd tink I wuz a pimp or somethin'. Everybody knows me knows I ain't. A pimp don't hold no job. I'm a bartender. Dem tarts, Margie and Poil, dey're just a side-line to pick up some extra dough. Strictly business like dey was fighters and I was deir manager, see? I fix the cops fer dem so's dey can hustle widhout gettin' pinched. Hell, dey'd be on de Island most of de time if it wasn't fer me. And I don't beat them up like a pimp would. I treat dem fine. Dey like me. We're pals, see? What if I do take deir dough? Dey'd on'y trow it away. Tarts can't hang on to dough. But I'm a bartender and I work hard for my livin' in dis dump. You know dat, Larry.

LARRY (*with inner sardonic amusement – flatteringly*). A shrewd business man, who doesn't miss any opportunity to get on in the world. That's what I'd call you.

ROCKY (*pleased*). Sure ting. Dat's me. Grab another ball, Larry.

LARRY *pours a drink from the bottle on* WILLIE's *table and gulps it down.* ROCKY *glances around the room.*

Yuh'd never tink all dese bums had a good bed upstairs to go to. Scared if dey hit the hay dey wouldn't be here when Hickey showed up, and dey'd miss a coupla drinks. Dat's what kept you up too, ain't it?

LARRY. It is. But not so much the hope of booze, if you can believe that. I've got the blues and Hickey's a great one to make a joke of everything and cheer you up.

ROCKY. Yeah, some kidder! Remember how he woiks up dat gag about his wife, when he's cockeyed, cryin' over her picture and den springin' it on yuh all of a sudden dat he left her in de hay wid de iceman? (*He laughs.*) I wonder what's happened to him. Yuh could set your watch by his periodicals before dis. Always got here a coupla days before Harry's birthday party, and now he's on'y got till tonight to make it. I hope he shows soon. Dis dump is like de morgue wid all dese bums passed out.

WILLIE OBAN *jerks and twitches in his sleep and begins to mumble. They watch him.*

WILLIE (*blurts from his dream*). It's a lie! (*Miserably.*) Papa! Papa!

LARRY. Poor devil. (*Then angry with himself.*) But to hell with pity! It does no good. I'm through with it!

ROCKY. Dreamin' about his old man. From what de old-timers say, de old gent sure made a p-ile of dough in de bucket-shop game before de cops got him. (*He considers* WILLIE *frowningly.*) Jees, I've seen him bad before but never dis bad. Look at dat get-up. Been playin' de old reliever game. Sold his suit and shoes at Solly's two days ago. Solly give him two bucks and a bum outfit. Yesterday he sells de bum one back to Solly for four bits and gets dese rags to put on. Now he's through. Dat's Solly's final edition he wouldn't take back for nuttin'. Willie sure is on de bottom. I ain't never seen no one so bad, except Hickey on de end of a coupla his bats.

LARRY (*sardonically*). It's a great game, the pursuit of happiness.

ROCKY. Harry don't know what to do about him. He called up his old lady's lawyer like he always does when Willie gets licked. Yuh remember dey used to send down a private dick to give him the rush to a cure, but de lawyer tells Harry nix, de old lady's off of Willie for keeps dis time and he can go to hell.

LARRY (*watches* WILLIE, *who is shaking in his sleep like an old dog*). There's the consolation that he hasn't far to go!

As if replying to this, WILLIE *comes to a crisis of jerks and moans.* LARRY *adds in a comically intense, crazy whisper.*

Be God, he's knocking on the door right now!

WILLIE (*suddenly yells in his nightmare*). It's a God-damned lie! (*He begins to sob.*) Oh, Papa! Jesus!

All the occupants of the room stir on their chairs but none of them wakes up except HOPE.

ROCKY (*grabs* WILLIE's *shoulder and shakes him*). Hey, you! Nix! Cut out de noise!

WILLIE *opens his eyes to stare around him with a bewildered horror.*

HOPE (*opens one eye to peer over his spectacles – drowsily*). Who's that yelling?

ROCKY. Willie, Boss. De Brooklyn boys is after him.

HOPE (*querulously*). Well, why don't you give the poor feller a drink and keep him quiet? Bejees, can't I get a wink of sleep in my own back room?

ROCKY (*indignantly to* LARRY). Listen to that blind-eyed, deef old bastard, will yuh? He give me strict orders not to let Willie hang up no more drinks, no matter –

HOPE (*mechanically puts a hand to his ear in the gesture of deafness*). What's that? I can't hear you. (*Then drowsily irascible.*) You're a cockeyed liar. Never refused a drink to anyone needed it bad in my life! Told you to use your judgment. Ought to know better. You're too busy thinking up ways to cheat me. Oh, I ain't as blind as you think. I can still see a cash register, bejees!

ROCKY (*grins at him affectionately now – flatteringly*). Sure, Boss. Swell chance of foolin' you!

HOPE. I'm wise to you and your sidekick, Chuck. Bejees, you're burglars, not barkeeps! Blind-eyed, deef old bastard, am I? Oh, I heard you! Heard you often when you didn't think. You and Chuck laughing behind my back, telling people you throw the money up in the air and whatever sticks to the ceiling is my share! A fine couple of crooks! You'd steal the pennies off your dead mother's eyes!

ROCKY (*winks at* LARRY). Aw, Harry, me and Chuck was on'y kiddin'.

HOPE (*more drowsily*). I'll fire both of you. Bejees, if you think you can play me for an easy mark, you've come to the wrong house. No one ever played Harry Hope for a sucker!

ROCKY (*to* LARRY). No one but everybody.

HOPE (*his eyes shut again – mutters*). Least you could do – keep things quiet – (*He falls asleep.*)

WILLIE (*pleadingly*). Give me a drink, Rocky. Harry said it was all right. God, I need a drink.

ROCKY. Den grab it. It's right under your nose.

WILLIE (*avidly*). Thanks. (*He takes the bottle with both twitching hands and tilts it to his lips and gulps down the whisky in big swallows.*)

ROCKY (*sharply*). When! When! (*He grabs the bottle.*) I didn't say, take a bath! (*Showing the bottle to* LARRY – *indignantly.*) Jees, look! He's killed a half pint or more!

He turns on WILLIE *angrily, but* WILLIE *has closed his eyes and is sitting quietly, shuddering, waiting for the effect.*

LARRY (*with a pitying glance*). Leave him be, the poor devil. A half pint of that dynamite in one swig will fix him for a while – if it doesn't kill him.

ROCKY (*shrugs his shoulders and sits down again*). Aw right by me. It ain't my booze.

Behind him, in the chair at left of the middle table, JOE MOTT, *the Negro, has been waking up.*

JOE (*his eyes blinking sleepily*). Whose booze? Gimme some. I don't care whose. Where's Hickey? Ain't he come yet? What time's it, Rocky?

ROCKY. Gettin' near time to open up. Time you begun to sweep up in de bar.

JOE (*lazily*). Never mind de time. If Hickey ain't come, it's time Joe goes to sleep again. I was dreamin' Hickey come in de door, crackin' one of dem drummer's jokes, wavin' a big bankroll and we was all goin' be drunk for two weeks. Wake up and no luck. (*Suddenly his eyes open wide.*) Wait a minute, dough. I got idea. Say, Larry, how 'bout dat young guy, Parritt came to look you up last night and rented a room? Where's he at?

LARRY. Up in his room, asleep. No hope in him, anyway, Joe. He's broke.

JOE. Dat what he told you? Me and Rocky knows different. Had
a roll when he paid you his room rent, didn't he, Rocky? I seen
it.

ROCKY. Yeah. He flashed it like he forgot and den tried to hide
it quick.

LARRY (*surprised and resentful*). He did, did he?

ROCKY. Yeah, I figgered he don't belong, but he said he was a
friend of yours.

LARRY. He's a liar. I wouldn't know him if he hadn't told me
who he was. His mother and I were friends years ago on the
Coast. (*He hesitates – then lowering his voice.*) You've read in the
papers about that bombing on the Coast when several people
got killed? Well, the one woman they pinched, Rosa Parritt, is
his mother. They'll be coming up for trial soon, and there's no
chance for them. She'll get life, I think. I'm telling you this so
you'll know why if Don acts a bit queer, and not jump on him.
He must be hard hit. He's her only kid.

ROCKY (*nods – then thoughtfully*). Why ain't he out dere stickin' by
her?

LARRY (*frowns*). Don't ask questions. Maybe there's a good
reason.

ROCKY (*stares at him – understandingly*). Sure. I get it. (*Then
wonderingly.*) But den what kind of a sap is he to hang on to his
right name?

LARRY (*irritably*). I'm telling you I don't know anything and I
don't want to know. To hell with the Movement and all
connected with it! I'm out of it, and everything else, and
damned glad to be.

ROCKY (*shrugs his shoulders – indifferently*). Well, don't tink I'm
interested in dis Parritt guy. He's nuttin' to me.

JOE. Me neider. If dere's one ting more'n annuder I cares nuttin
about, it's de sucker game you and Hugo call de Movement.
(*He chuckles – reminiscently,*) Reminds me of damn fool argumen†
me and Mose Porter has de udder night. He's drunk and I'm
drunker. He says, 'Socialist and Anarchist, we ought to shoot
dem dead. Dey's all no-good sons of bitches.' I says, 'Hold on,
you talk 's if Anarchists and Socialists was de same.' 'Dey is,' he
says. 'Dey's both no-good bastards.' 'No, dey ain't,' I says. 'I'll
explain the difference. De Anarchist he never works. He drinks
but he never buys, and if he do ever get a nickel, he blows it in

on bombs, and he wouldn't give you nothin'. So go ahead and shoot him. But de Socialist, sometimes, he's got a job, and if he gets ten bucks, he's bound by his religion to split fifty-fifty wid you. You say – how about my cut, Comrade? And you gets de five. So you don't shoot no Socialists while I'm around. Dat is, not if they got anything. Of course, if dey's broke, den dey's no-good bastards, too.' (*He laughs, immensely tickled.*)

LARRY (*grins with sardonic appreciation*). Be God, Joe, you've got all the beauty of human nature and the practical wisdom of the world in that little parable.

ROCKY (*winks at* JOE). Sure, Larry ain't de on'y wise guy in dis dump, hey, Joe?

At a sound from the hall he turns as DON PARRITT *appears in the doorway.* ROCKY *speaks to* LARRY *out of the side of his mouth.*

Here's your guy.

PARRITT *comes forward. He is eighteen, tall and broad-shouldered but thin, gangling and awkward. His face is good-looking, with blond curly hair and large regular features but his personality is unpleasant. There is a shifting defiance and ingratiation in his light-blue eyes and an irritating aggressiveness in his manner. His clothes and shoes are new, comparatively expensive, sporty in style. He looks as though he belonged in a pool room patronized by would-be sports. He glances around defensively, sees* LARRY *and comes forward.*

PARRITT. Hello, Larry. (*He nods to* ROCKY *and* JOE.) Hello.

They nod and size him up with expressionless eyes.

LARRY (*without cordiality*). What's up? I thought you'd be asleep.

PARRITT. Couldn't make it. I got sick of lying awake. Thought I might as well see if you were around.

LARRY (*indicates the chair on the right of table*). Sit down and join the bums then.

PARRITT *sits down.* LARRY *adds meaningfully.*

The rules of the house are that drinks may be served at all hours.

PARRITT (*forcing a smile*). I get you, But hell, I'm just about broke (*He catches* ROCKY'*s and* JOE'*s contemptuous glances – quickly.*) Oh, I know you guys saw – You think I've got a roll. Well, you're all wrong. I'll show you. (*He takes a small wad of dollar bills from his pocket.*) It's all ones. And I've got to live on it till I get a job. (*Then with defensive truculence.*) You think I fixed up a phony, don't you? Why the hell would I? Where would I get a real roll? You don't get rich doing what I've been doing. Ask Larry. You're lucky in the Movement if you have enough to eat.

LARRY *regards him puzzledly.*

ROCKY (*coldly*). What's de song and dance about? We ain't said nuttin'.

PARRITT (*lamely – placating them now*). Why, I was just putting you right. But I don't want you to think I'm a tightwad. I'll buy a drink if you want one.

JOE (*cheering up*). If? Man, when I don't want a drink, you call de morgue, tell dem come take Joe's body away, 'cause he's sure enuf dead. Gimme de bottle quick, Rocky, before he changes his mind!

ROCKY *passes him the bottle and glass. He pours a brimful drink and tosses it down his throat, and hands the bottle and glass to* LARRY.

ROCKY. I'll take a cigar when I go in de bar. What're you havin'?

PARRITT. Nothing. I'm on the wagon. What's the damage? (*He holds out a dollar bill.*)

ROCKY. Fifteen cents. (*He makes change from his pocket.*)

PARRITT. Must be some booze!

LARRY. It's cyanide cut with carbolic acid to give it a mellow flavour. Here's luck! (*He drinks.*)

ROCKY. Guess I'll get back in de bar and catch a coupla winks before opening-up time. (*He squeezes through the tables and disappears, right-rear, behind the curtain. In the section of bar at right, he comes forward and sits at the table and slumps back, closing his eyes and yawning.*)

JOE (*stares calculatingly at* PARRITT *and then looks away – aloud to himself, philosophically*). One-drink guy. Dat well done run dry. No hope till Harry's birthday party. 'Less Hickey shows up. (*He turns to* LARRY.) If Hickey comes, Larry, you wake me up if you has to bat me wid a chair. (*He settles himself and immediately falls asleep.*)

PARRITT. Who's Hickey?

LARRY. A hardware drummer. An old friend of Harry Hope's and all the gang. He's a grand guy. He comes here twice a year regularly on a periodical drunk and blows in all his money.

PARRITT (*with a disparaging glance around*). Must be hard up for a place to hang out.

LARRY. It has its points for him. He never runs into anyone he knows in his business here.

PARRITT (*lowering his voice*). Yes, that's what I want, too. I've got to stay under cover, Larry, like I told you last night.

LARRY. You did a lot of hinting. You didn't tell me anything.

PARRITT. You can guess, can't you? (*He changes the subject abruptly.*) I've been in some dumps on the Coast, but this is the limit. What kind of joint is it, anyway?

LARRY (*with a sardonic grin*). What is it? It's the No Chance Saloon. It's Bedrock Bar, The End of the Line Café, The Bottom of the Sea Rathskeller! Don't you notice the beautiful calm in the atmosphere? That's because it's the last harbour. No one here has to worry about where they're going next, because there is no farther they can go. It's a great comfort to them. Although even here they keep up the appearances of life with a few harmless pipe dreams about their yesterdays and tomorrows, as you'll see for yourself if you're here long.

PARRITT (*stares at him curiously*). What's your pipe dream, Larry?

LARRY (*hiding resentment*). Oh, I'm the exception. I haven't any left, thank God. (*Shortly.*) Don't complain about this place. You couldn't find a better for lying low.

PARRITT. I'm glad of that, Larry. I don't feel any too damned good. I was knocked off my base by that business on the Coast, and since then it's been no fun dodging around the country, thinking every guy you see might be a dick.

LARRY (*sympathetically now*). No, it wouldn't be. But you're safe here. The cops ignore this dump. They think it's as harmless as a graveyard. (*He grins sardonically.*) And, be God, they're right.

PARRITT. It's been lonely as hell. (*Impulsively.*) Christ, Larry, I was glad to find you. I kept saying to myself, 'If I can only find Larry. He's the one guy in the world who can understand –' (*He hesitates, staring at* LARRY *with a strange appeal.*)

LARRY (*watching him puzzledly*). Understand what?

PARRITT (*hastily*). Why, all I've been through. (*Looking away.*) Oh, I know you're thinking, This guy has a hell of a nerve. I haven't seen him since he was a kid. I'd forgotten he was alive.

But I've never forgotten you, Larry. You were the only friend
of Mother's who ever paid attention to me, or knew I was alive.
All the others were too busy with the Movement. Even Mother.
And I had no Old Man. You used to take me on your knee and
tell me stories and crack jokes and make me laugh. You'd ask
me questions and take what I said seriously. I guess I got to
feel in the years you lived with us that you'd taken the place of
my Old Man. (*Embarrassedly.*) But, hell, that sounds like a lot of
mush. I suppose you don't remember a damned thing about it.

LARRY (*moved in spite of himself*). I remember well. You were a
serious lonely little shaver. (*Then, resenting being moved, changes
the subject.*) How is it they didn't pick you up when they got
your mother and the rest?

PARRITT (*in a lowered voice but eagerly, as if he wanted this chance to
tell about it*). I wasn't around, and as soon as I heard the news I
went under cover. You've noticed my glad rags. I was staked to
them – as a disguise, sort of. I hung around pool rooms and
gambling joints and hooker shops, where they'd never look for
a Wobblie, pretending I was a sport. Anyway, they'd grabbed
everyone important, so I suppose they didn't think of me until
afterward.

LARRY. The papers say the cops got them all dead to rights, that
the Burns dicks knew every move before it was made, and
someone inside the Movement must have sold out and tipped
them off.

PARRITT (*turns to look* LARRY *in the eyes – slowly*). Yes, I guess
that must be true, Larry. It hasn't come out who it was. It may
never come out. I suppose whoever it was made a bargain with
the Burns men to keep him out of it. They won't need his
evidence.

LARRY (*tensely*). By God, I hate to believe it of any of the crowd,
if I am through long since with any connection with them. I
know they're damned fools, most of them, as stupidly greedy
for power as the worst capitalist they attack, but I'd swear there
couldn't be a yellow stool pigeon among them.

PARRITT. Sure. I'd have sworn that, too, Larry.

LARRY. I hope his soul rots in hell, whoever it is!

PARRITT. Yes, so do I.

LARRY (*after a pause – shortly*). How did you locate me? I hoped
I'd found a place of retirement here where no one in the
Movement would ever come to disturb my peace.

PARRITT. I found out through Mother.

LARRY. I asked her not to tell anyone.

PARRITT. She didn't tell me, but she'd kept all your letters and I found where she'd hidden them in the flat. I sneaked up there one night after she was arrested.

LARRY. I'd never have thought she was a woman who'd keep letters.

PARRITT. No, I wouldn't either. There's nothing soft or sentimental about Mother.

LARRY. I never answered her last letters. I haven't written her in a couple of years – or anyone else. I've gotten beyond the desire to communicate with the world – or, what's more to the point, let it bother me any more with its greedy madness.

PARRITT. It's funny Mother kept in touch with you so long. When she's finished with anyone, she's finished. She's always been proud of that. And you know how she feels about the Movement. Like a revivalist preacher about religion. Anyone who loses faith in it is more than dead to her; he's a Judas who ought to be boiled in oil. Yet she seemed to forgive you.

LARRY (sardonically). She didn't, don't worry. She wrote to denounce me and try to bring the sinner to repentance and a belief in the One True Faith again.

PARRITT. What made you leave the Movement, Larry? Was it on account of Mother?

LARRY (starts). Don't be a damned fool! What the hell put that in your head?

PARRITT. Why, nothing – except I remember what a fight you had with her before you left.

LARRY (resentfully). Well, if you do, I don't. That was eleven years ago. You were only seven. If we did quarrel, it was because I told her I'd become convinced the Movement was only a beautiful pipe dream.

PARRITT (with a strange smile). I don't remember it that way.

LARRY. Then you can blame your imagination – and forget it. (He changes the subject abruptly.) You asked me why I quit the Movement. I had a lot of good reasons. One was myself, and another was my comrades, and the last was the breed of swine called men in general. For myself, I was forced to admit, at the end of thirty years' devotion to the Cause, that I was never

made for it. I was born condemned to be one of those who has
to see all sides of a question. When you're damned like that,
the questions multiply for you until in the end it's all question
and no answer. As history proves, to be a worldly success at
anything, especially revolution, you have to wear blinders like a
horse and see only straight in front of you. You have to see,
too, that this is all black, and that is all white. As for my
comrades in the Great Cause, I felt as Horace Walpole did
about England, that he could love it if it weren't for the people
in it. The material the ideal free society must be constructed
from is men themselves and you can't build a marble temple
out of a mixture of mud and manure. When man's soul isn't a
sow's ear, it will be time enough to dream of silk purses. (*He
chuckles sardonically – then irritably as if suddenly provoked at himself
for talking so much.*) Well, that's why I quit the Movement, if it
leaves you any wiser. At any rate, you see it had nothing to do
with your mother.

PARRITT (*smiles almost mockingly*). Oh, sure, I see. But I'll bet
Mother has always thought it was on her account. You know
her, Larry. To hear her go on sometimes, you'd think she was
the Movement.

LARRY (*stares at him, puzzled and repelled – sharply*). That's a hell
of a way for you to talk, after what happened to her!

PARRITT (*at once confused and guilty*). Don't get me wrong. I
wasn't sneering, Larry. Only kidding. I've said the same thing
to her lots of times to kid her. But you're right. I know I
shouldn't now. I keep forgetting she's in jail. It doesn't seem
real. I can't believe it about her. She's always been so free. I –
But I don't want to think of it. (LARRY *is moved to a puzzled pity
in spite of himself.* PARRITT *changes the subject.*) What have you
been doing all the years since you left – the Coast, Larry?

LARRY (*sardonically*). Nothing I could help doing. If I don't
believe in the Movement, I don't believe in anything else either,
especially not the State. I've refused to become a useful
member of its society. I've been a philosophical drunken bum,
and proud of it. (*Abruptly his tone sharpens with resentful warning.*)
Listen to me. I hope you've deduced that I've my own reason
for answering the impertinent questions of a stranger, for that's
all you are to me. I have a strong hunch you've come here
expecting something of me. I'm warning you, at the start, so
there'll be no misunderstanding, that I've nothing left to give,
and I want to be left alone, and I'll thank you to keep your life
to yourself. I feel you're looking for some answer to something.

I have no answer to give anyone, not even myself. Unless you can call what Heine wrote in his poem to morphine an answer. (*He quotes a translation of the closing couplet sardonically.*)

Lo, sleep is good; better is death; in sooth,
The best of all were never to be born.

PARRITT (*shrinks a bit frightenedly*). That's the hell of an answer. (*Then with a forced grin of bravado.*) Still, you never know when it might come in handy. (*He looks away.*)

LARRY *stares at him puzzledly, interested in spite of himself and at the same time vaguely uneasy.*

LARRY (*forcing a casual tone*). I don't suppose you've had much chance to hear news of your mother since she's been in jail?

PARRITT. No. No chance. (*He hesitates – then blurts out.*) Anyway, I don't think she wants to hear from me. We had a fight just before that business happened. She bawled me out because I was going around with tarts. That got my goat, coming from her. I told her, 'You've always acted the free woman, you've never let anything stop you from –' (*He checks himself – goes on hurriedly.*) That made her sore. She said she wouldn't give a damn what I did except she'd begun to suspect I was too interested in outside things and losing interest in the Movement.

LARRY (*stares at him*). And were you?

PARRITT (*hesitates – then with intensity*). Sure I was! I'm no damned fool! I couldn't go on believing forever that gang was going to change the world by shooting off their loud traps on soapboxes and sneaking around blowing up a lousy building or a bridge! I got wise it was all a crazy pipe dream! (*Appealingly.*) The same as you did, Larry. That's why I came to you. I knew you'd understand. What finished me was this last business of someone selling out. How can you believe anything after a thing like that happens? It knocks you cold! You don't know what the hell is what! You're through! (*Appealingly,*) You know how I feel, don't you, Larry?

LARRY *stares at him, moved by sympathy and pity in spite of himself, disturbed, and resentful at being disturbed, and puzzled by something he feels about PARRITT that isn't right. But before he can reply, HUGO suddenly raises his head from his arms in a half-awake alcoholic daze and speaks.*

HUGO (*quotes aloud to himself in a gutteral declamatory style*). 'The days grow hot, O Babylon! 'Tis cool beneath thy villow trees!'

PARRITT *turns startledly as* HUGO *peers muzzily without recognition at him.* HUGO *exclaims automatically in his tone of denunciation.*

Gottammed stool pigeon!

PARRITT (*shrinks away – stammers*). What? Who do you mean? (*Then furiously.*) You lousy bum, you can't call me that! (*He draws back his fist.*)

HUGO (*ignores this – recognizing him now, bursts into his childish teasing giggle*). Hellow, leedle Don! Leedle monkey-face. I did not recognize you. You have grown big boy. How is your mother? Where you come from? (*He breaks into his wheedling, bullying tone.*) Don't be a fool! Loan me a dollar! Buy me a trink! (*As if this exhausted him, he abruptly forgets it and plumps his head down on his arms again and is asleep.*)

PARRITT (*with eager relief*). Sure, I'll buy you a drink Hugo. I'm broke, but I can afford one for you. I'm sorry I got sore. I ought to have remembered when you're soused you call everyone a stool pigeon. But it's no damned joke right at this time. (*He turns to* LARRY, *who is regarding him now fixedly with an uneasy expression as if he suddenly were afraid of his own thoughts – forcing a smile.*) Gee, he's passed out again. (*He stiffens defensively.*) What are you giving me the hard look for? Oh, I know. You thought I was going to hit him? What do you think I am? I've always had a lot of respect for Hugo. I've always stood up for him when people in the Movement panned him for an old drunken has-been. He had the guts to serve ten years in the can in his own country and get his eyes ruined in solitary. I'd like to see some of them here stick that. Well, they'll get a chance now to show – (*Hastily.*) I don't mean – But let's forget that. Tell me some more about this dump. Who are all these tanks? Who's that guy trying to catch pneumonia? (*He indicates* LEWIS.)

LARRY (*stares at him almost frightenedly – then looks away and grasps eagerly this chance to change the subject. He begins to describe the sleepers with sardonic relish but at the same time showing his affection for them*). That's Captain Lewis, a one-time hero of the British Army. He strips to display that scar on his back he got from a native spear whenever he's completely plastered. The bewhiskered bloke opposite him is General Wetjoen, who led a commando in the War. The two of them met when they came here to work in the Boer War spectacle at the St Louis Fair and they've been bosom pals ever since. They dream the hours

away in happy dispute over the brave days in South Africa
when they tried to murder each other. The little guy between
them was in it, too, as correspondent for some English paper.
His nickname here is Jimmy Tomorrow. He's the leader of our
Tomorrow Movement.

PARRITT. What do they do for a living?

LARRY. As little as possible. Once in a while one of them makes
a successful touch somewhere and some of them get a few
dollars a month from connections at home, who pay it on
condition they never come back. For the rest, they live on free
lunch and their old friend, Harry Hope, who doesn't give a
damn what anyone does or doesn't do, as long as he likes you.

PARRITT. It must be a tough life.

LARRY. It's not. Don't waste your pity. They wouldn't thank you
for it. They manage to get drunk, by hook or crook, and keep
their pipe dreams, and that's all they ask of life. I've never
known more contented men. It isn't often that men attain the
true goal of their heart's desire. The same applies to Harry
himself and his two cronies at the far table. He's so satisfied
with life he's never set foot out of this place since his wife died
twenty years ago. He has no need of the outside world at all.
This place has a fine trade from the Market people across the
street and the waterfront workers, so in spite of Harry's thirst
and his generous heart, he comes out even. He never worries
in hard times because there's always old friends from the days
when he was a jitney Tammany politician, and a friendly
brewery to tide him over. Don't ask me what his two pals work
at because they don't. Except at being his lifetime guests. The
one facing this way is his brother-in-law, Ed Mosher, who once
worked for a circus in the ticket wagon. Pat McGloin, the other
one, was a police lieutenant back in the flush times of graft
when everything went. But he got too greedy and when the
usual reform investigation came he was caught red-handed and
thrown off the Force. (*He nods at* JOE.) Joe here has a
yesterday in the same flush period. He ran a coloured
gambling-house then and was a hell of a sport, so they say.
Well that's our whole family circle of inmates, except the two
barkeeps and their girls, three ladies of the pavement that
room on the third floor.

PARRITT (*bitterly*). To hell with them! I never want to see a
whore again! (*As* LARRY *flashes him a puzzled glance, he adds
confusedly.*) I mean, they always get you in dutch.

While he is speaking WILLIE OBAN *has opened his eyes. He leans toward them, drunk now from the effect of the huge drink he took, and speaks with a mocking suavity.*

WILLIE. Why omit me from your Who's Who in Dypsomania, Larry? An unpardonable slight, especially as I am the only inmate of royal blood. (*To* PARRITT – *ramblingly.*) Educated at Harvard, too. You must have noticed the atmosphere of culture here. My humble contribution. Yes, Generous Stranger – I trust you're generous – I was born in the purple, the son, but unfortunately not the heir, of the late world-famous Bill Oban, King of the Bucket Shops. A revolution deposed him, conducted by the District Attorney. He was sent into exile. In fact, not to mince matters, they locked him in the can and threw away the key. Alas, his was an adventurous spirit that pined in confinement. And so he died. Forgive these reminiscences. Undoubtedly all this is well known to you. Everyone in the world knows.

PARRITT (*uncomfortably*). Tough luck. No, I never heard of him.

WILLIE (*blinks at him incredulously*). Never heard? I thought everyone in the world – Why, even at Harvard I discovered my father was well known by reputation, although that was some time before the District Attorney gave him so much unwelcome publicity. Yes, even as a freshman I was notorious. I was accepted socially with all the warm cordiality that Henry Wadsworth Longfellow would have shown a drunken Negress dancing the can can at high noon on Brattle Street. Harvard was my father's idea. He was an ambitious man. Dictatorial, too. Always knowing what was best for me. But I did make myself a brilliant student. A dirty trick on my classmates, inspired by revenge, I fear. (*He quotes.*) 'Dear college days, with pleasure rife! The grandest gladdest days of life!' But, of course, that is a Yale hymn, and they're given to rah-rah exaggeration at New Haven. I was a brilliant student at Law School, too. My Father wanted a lawyer in the family. He was a calculating man. A thorough knowledge of the law close at hand in the house to help him find fresh ways to evade it. But I discovered the loophole of whisky and escaped his jurisdiction. (*Abruptly to* PARRITT.) Speaking of whisky, sir, reminds me – and, I hope, reminds you – that when meeting a Prince the customary salutation is 'What'll you have?'

PARRITT (*with defensive resentment*). Nix! All you guys seem to think I'm made of dough. Where would I get the coin to blow everyone?

WILLIE (*sceptically*). Broke? You haven't the thirsty look of the impecunious. I'd judge you to be a plutocrat, your pockets stuffed with ill-gotten gains. Two or three dollars, at least. And don't think we will question how you got it. As Vespasian remarked, the smell of all whisky is sweet.

PARRITT. What do you mean, how I got it? (*To* LARRY, *forcing a laugh*.) It's a laugh, calling me a plutocrat, isn't it, Larry, when I've been in the Movement all my life.

LARRY *gives him an uneasy suspicious glance, then looks away, as if avoiding something he does not wish to see.*

WILLIE (*disgustedly*). Ah, one of those, eh? I believe you now, all right! Go away and blow yourself up, that's a good lad. Hugo is the only licensed preacher of that gospel here. A dangerous terrorist, Hugo! He would as soon blow the collar off a schooner of beer as look at you! (*To* LARRY.) Let us ignore this useless youth, Larry. Let us join in prayer that Hickey, the Great Salesman, will soon arrive bringing the blessed bourgeois long green! Would that Hickey or Death would come! Meanwhile, I will sing a song. A beautiful old New England folk ballad which I picked up at Harvard amid the debris of education. (*He sings in a boisterous baritone, rapping on the table with his knuckles at the indicated spots in the song.*)

Jack, oh, Jack, was a sailor lad
And he came to a tavern for gin.
He rapped and he rapped with a (*Rap, rap, rap.*)
But never a soul seemed in.

The drunks at the tables stir. ROCKY *gets up from his chair in the bar and starts back for the entrance to the back room.* HOPE *cocks one irritable eye over his specs.* JOE MOTT *opens both of his and grins.* WILLIE *interposes some drunken whimsical exposition to* LARRY.

The origin of this beautiful ditty is veiled in mystery, Larry. There was a legend bruited about in Cambridge lavatories that Waldo Emerson composed it during his uninformative period as a minister, while he was trying to write a sermon. But my own opinion is, it goes back much further, and Jonathan Edwards was the author of both words and music. (*He sings.*)

He rapped and rapped, and tapped and tapped
Enough to wake the dead
Till he heard a damsel (*Rap, rap, rap.*)
On a window right over his head.

The drunks are blinking their eyes now, grumbling and cursing.

ROCKY *appears from the bar at rear, right, yawning.*

HOPE (*with fuming irritation*). Rocky! Bejees, can't you keep that crazy bastard quiet?

ROCKY *starts for* WILLIE.

WILLIE. And now the influence of a good woman enters our mariner's life. Well, perhaps 'good' isn't the word. But very, very kind. (*He sings.*)

'Oh, come up,' she cried, 'my sailor lad,
And you and I'll agree.
And I'll show you the prettiest (*Rap, rap, rap.*)
That ever you did see.'

(*He speaks.*) You see, Larry? The lewd Puritan touch, obviously, and it grows more marked as we go on. (*He sings.*)

Oh, he put his arm around her waist,
He gazed in her bright blue eyes
And then he –

But here ROCKY *shakes him roughly by the shoulder.*

ROCKY. Piano! What d'yuh tink dis dump is, a dump?

HOPE. Give him the bum's rush upstairs! Lock him in his room!

ROCKY (*yanks* WILLIE *by the arm*). Come on, Bum.

WILLIE (*dissolves into pitiable terror*). No! Please, Rocky! I'll go crazy up in that room alone! It's haunted! I – (*He calls to* HOPE.) Please, Harry! Let me stay here! I'll be quiet!

HOPE (*immediately relents – indignantly*). What the hell you doing to him, Rocky? I didn't tell you to beat up the poor guy. Leave him alone, long as he's quiet.

ROCKY *lets go of* WILLIE *disgustedly and goes back to his chair in the bar.*

WILLIE (*huskily*). Thanks, Harry. You're a good scout. (*He closes his eyes and sinks back in his chair exhaustedly, twitching and quivering again.*)

HOPE (*addressing* MCGLOIN *and* MOSHER, *who are sleepily awake – accusingly*). Always the way. Can't trust nobody. Leave it to that Dago to keep order and it's like bedlam in a cathouse, singing and everything. And you two big barflies are a hell of a help to me, ain't you? Eat and sleep and get drunk! All you're good for bejees! Well, you can take that 'I'll-have-the-same' look off your maps! There ain't going to be no more drinks on the house till hell freezes over! (*Neither of the two is impressed either by his insults or his threats. They grin hangover grins of tolerant affection at him and wink at each other.* HARRY *fumes.*) Yeah, grin! Wink, bejees! Fine pair of sons of bitches to have glued on me for life!

But he can't get a rise out of them and he subsides into a fuming mumble. Meanwhile, at the middle table, CAPTAIN LEWIS *and* GENERAL WETJOEN *are as wide awake as heavy hangovers permit.* JIMMY TOMORROW *nods, his eyes blinking.* LEWIS *is gazing across the table at* JOE MOTT, *who is still chuckling to himself over* WILLIE's *song. The expression on* LEWIS's *face is that of one who can't believe his eyes.*

LEWIS (*aloud to himself, with a muzzy wonder*). Good God! Have I been drinking at the same table with a bloody Kaffir?

JOE (*grinning*). Hello, Captain. You comin' up for air? Kaffir? Who's he?

WETJOEN (*blurrily*). Kaffir, dot's a nigger, Joe.

JOE *stiffens and his eyes narrow.* WETJOEN *goes on with heavy jocosity.*

Dot's joke on him, Joe. He don't know you. He's still plind drunk, the ploody Limey chentleman! A great mistake I missed him at the pattle of Modder River. Vit mine rifle I shoot damn fool Limey officers py the dozen, but him I miss. De pity of it! (*He chuckles and slaps* LEWIS *on his bare shoulder.*) Hey, wake up, Cecil, you ploody fool! Don't you know your old friend, Joe? He's no damned Kaffir! He's white, Joe is!

LEWIS (*light dawning – contritely*). My profound apologies, Joseph, old chum. Eyesight a trifle blurry, I'm afraid. Whitest coloured man I ever knew. Proud to call you my friend. No hard feelings, what? (*He holds out his hand.*)

JOE (*at once grins good-naturedly and shakes his hand*). No, Captain, I know it's mistake. Youse regular, if you is a Limey. (*Then his face hardening.*) But I don't stand for 'nigger' from nobody. Never did. In de old days, people calls me 'nigger' wakes up in de hospital. I was de leader ob de Dirty Half-Dozen Gang. All six of us coloured boys, we was tough and I was de toughest.

WETJOEN (*inspired to boastful reminiscence*). Me, in old days in Transvaal, I vas so tough and strong I grab axle of ox wagon mit full load and lift like feather.

LEWIS (*smiling amiably*). As for you, my balmy Boer that walks like a man, I say again it was a grave error in our foreign

policy ever to set you free, once we nabbed you and your
commando with Cronje. We should have taken you to the
London zoo and incarcerated you in the baboons' cage. With a
sign: 'Spectators may distinguish the true baboon by his blue
behind.'

WETJOEN (*grins*). Gott! To dink, ten better Limey officers, at
least, I shoot clean in the mittle of forehead at Spion Kopje,
and you I miss! I neffer forgive myself!

JIMMY TOMORROW *blinks benignantly from one to the other with
a gentle drunken smile.*

JIMMY (*sentimentally*). Now, come, Cecil, Piet! We must forget the
War. Boer and Briton, each fought fairly and played the game
till the better man won and then we shook hands. We are all
brothers within the Empire united beneath the flag on which
the sun never sets. (*Tears come to his eyes. He quotes with great
sentiment, if with slight application.*) 'Ship me somewhere east of
Suez –'

LARRY (*breaks in sardonically*). Be God, you're there already,
Jimmy. Worst is best here, and East is West, and tomorrow is
yesterday. What more do you want?

JIMMY (*with bleary benevolence, shaking his head in mild rebuke*). No,
Larry, old friend, you can't deceive me. You pretend a bitter,
cynic philosophy, but in your heart you are the kindest man
among us.

LARRY (*disconcerted – irritably*). The hell you say!

PARRITT (*leans toward him – confidentially*). What a bunch of
cuckoos!

JIMMY (*as if reminded of something – with a pathetic attempt at a
brisk, no-more-nonsense air*). Tomorrow, yes. It's high time I
straightened out and got down to business again. (*He brushes his
sleeve fastidiously.*) I must have this suit cleaned and pressed. I
can't look like a tramp when I –

JOE (*who has been brooding – interrupts*). Yes, suh, white folks
always said I was white. In de days when I was flush, Joe Mott's
de only coloured man dey allows in de white gamblin' houses.
'You're all right, Joe, you're white,' dey says. (*He chuckles.*)
Wouldn't let me play craps, dough. Dey know I could make
dem dice behave. 'Any odder game and any limit you like, Joe,'
dey says. Man, de money I lost! (*He chuckles – then with an
underlying defensiveness.*) Look at de Big Chief in dem days. He

knew I was white. I'd saved my dough so I could start my own gamblin' house. Folks in de know tells me, see de man at de top, den you never has trouble. You git Harry Hope give you a letter to de Chief. And Harry does. Don't you, Harry?

HOPE (*preoccupied with his own thoughts*). Eh? Sure. Big Bill was a good friend of mine. I had plenty of friends high up in those days. Still could have if I wanted to go out and see them. Sure, I gave you a letter. I said you was white. What the hell of it?

JOE (*to* CAPTAIN LEWIS, *who has relapsed into a sleepy daze and is listening to him with an absurd strained attention without comprehending a word*). Dere. You see, Captain. I went to see de Chief, shakin' in my boots, and dere he is sittin' behind a big desk, lookin' as big as a freight train. He don't look up. He keeps me waitin' and waitin', and after 'bout an hour, seems like to me, he says slow and quiet like dere wasn't no harm in him, 'You want to open a gamblin' joint, does you, Joe?' But he don't give me no time to answer. He jumps up, lookin' as big as two freight trains, and he pounds his fist like a ham on de desk, and he shouts, 'You black son of a bitch, Harry says you're white and you better be white or dere's a little iron room up de river waitin' for you!' Den he sits down and says quiet again, 'All right. You can open. Git de hell outa here!' So I opens, and he finds out I'se white sure 'nuff, 'cause I run wide open for years and pays my sugar on de dot, and de cops and I is friends. (*He chuckles with pride.*) Dem old days! Many's de night I come in here. Dis was a first-class hangout for sports in dem days. Good whisky, fifteen cents, two for two bits. I t'rows down a fifty-dollar bill like it was trash paper and says, 'Drink it up, boys, I don't want no change.' Ain't dat right, Harry?

HOPE (*caustically*). Yes, and bejees, if I ever seen you throw fifty cents on the bar now, I'd know I had delirium tremens! You've told that story ten million times and if I have to hear it again, that'll give me DTs anyway!

JOE (*chuckling*). Gettin' drunk every day for twenty years ain't give you de Brooklyn boys. You needn't be scared of me!

LEWIS (*suddenly turns and beams on* HOPE). Thank you, Harry, old chum. I will have a drink, now you mention it, seeing it's so near your birthday.

The others laugh.

HOPE (*puts his hand to his ear – angrily*). What's that? I can't hear you.

LEWIS (*sadly*). No, I fancied you wouldn't.

HOPE. I don't have to hear, bejees! Booze is the only thing you ever talk about!

LEWIS (*sadly*). True, Yet there was a time when my conversation was more comprehensive. But as I became burdened with years, it seemed rather pointless to discuss my other subject.

HOPE. You can't joke with me! How much room rent do you owe me, tell me that?

LEWIS. Sorry. Adding has always baffled me. Subtraction is my forte.

HOPE (*snarling*). Arrh! Think you're funny! Captain, bejees! Showing off your wounds! Put on your clothes, for Christ's sake! This ain't no Turkish bath! Lousy Limey army! Took 'em years to lick a gang of Dutch hayseeds!

WETJOEN. Dot's right, Harry. Gif him hell!

HOPE. No lip out of you, neither, you Dutch spinach! General, hell! Salvation Army, that's what you'd ought t'been General in! Bragging what a shot you were, and, bejees, you missed him! And he missed you, that's just as bad! And now the two of you bum on me! (*Threateningly.*) But you've broke the camel's back this time, bejees! You pay up tomorrow or out you go!

LEWIS (*earnestly*). My dear fellow, I give you my word of honour as an officer and a gentleman, you shall be paid tomorrow.

WETJOEN. Ve swear it, Harry! Tomorrow vidout fail!

MCGLOIN (*a twinkle in his eye*). There you are, Harry. Sure, what could be fairer?

MOSHER (*with a wink at* MCGLOIN). Yes, you can't ask more than that, Harry. A promise is a promise – as I've often discovered.

HOPE (*turns on them*). I mean the both of you, too! An old grafting flatfoot and a circus bunco steerer! Fine company for me, bejees! Couple of con men living in my flat since Christ knows when! Getting fat as hogs, too! And you ain't even got the decency to get me upstairs where I got a good bed! Let me sleep on a chair like a bum! Kept me down here waitin' for Hickey to show up, hoping I'd blow you to more drinks!

MCGLOIN. Ed and I did our damnedest to get you up, didn't we, Ed?

MOSHER. We did. But you said you couldn't bear the flat

because it was one of those nights when memory brought poor old Bessie back to you.

HOPE (*his face instantly becoming long and sad and sentimental – mournfully*). Yes, that's right, boys. I remember now. I could almost see her in every room just as she used to be – and it's twenty years since she – (*His throat and eyes fill up.*)

A suitable sentimental hush falls on the room.

LARRY (*in a sardonic whisper to* PARRITT). Isn't a pipe dream of yesterday a touching thing? By all accounts, Bessie nagged the hell out of him.

JIMMY (*who has been dreaming, a look of prim resolution on his face, speaks aloud to himself.*) No more of this sitting around and loafing. Time I took hold of myself. I must have my shoes soled and heeled and shined first thing tomorrow morning. A general spruce-up. I want to have a well-groomed appearance when I – (*His voice fades out as he stares in front of him.*)

No one pays any attention to him except LARRY *and* PARRITT.

LARRY (*as before, in a sardonic aside to* PARRITT). The tomorrow movement is a sad and beautiful thing, too!

MCGLOIN (*with a huge sentimental sigh – and a calculating look at* HOPE). Poor old Bessie! You don't find her like in these days. A sweeter woman never drew breath.

MOSHER (*in a similar calculating mood*). Good old Bess. A man couldn't want a better sister than she was to me.

HOPE (*mournfully*). Twenty years, and I've never set foot out of this house since the day I buried her. Didn't have the heart. Once she'd gone, I didn't give a damn for anything. I lost all my ambition. Without her, nothing seemed worth the trouble. You remember, Ed, you, too, Mac – the boys was going to nominate me for Alderman. It was all fixed. Bessie wanted it and she was so proud. But when she was taken, I told them, 'No boys', I can't do it. I simply haven't the heart. I'm through. I would have won the election easy, too. (*He says this a bit defiantly.*) Oh, I know there was jealous wise guys said the boys was giving me the nomination becaust they knew they couldn't win that year in this ward. But that's a damned lie! I knew every man, woman and child in the ward, almost. Bessie made me make friends with everyone, helped me remember all their names. I'd have been elected easy.

MCGLOIN. You would, Harry. It was a sure thing.

MOSHER. A dead cinch, Harry. Everyone knows that.

HOPE. Sure they do. But after Bessie died, I didn't have the
heart. Still, I know while she'd appreciate my grief, she
wouldn't want it to keep me cooped up in here all my life. So
I've made up my mind I'll go out soon. Take a walk around the
ward, see all the friends I used to know, get together with the
boys and maybe tell 'em I'll let 'em deal me a hand in their
game again. Yes, bejees, I'll do it. My birthday, tomorrow,
that'd be the right time to turn over a new leaf. Sixty. That
ain't too old.

MCGLOIN (*flatteringly*). It's the prime of life, Harry.

MOSHER. Wonderful thing about you, Harry, you keep young
as you ever was.

JIMMY (*dreaming aloud again*). Get my things from the laundry.
They must still have them. Clean collar and shirt. If I wash the
ones I've got on any more, they'll fall apart. Socks, too. I want
to make a good appearance. I met Dick Trumbull on the street
a year or two ago. He said. 'Jimmy, the publicity department's
never been the same since you got – resigned. It's dead as hell.'
I said. 'I know. I've heard rumours the management were at
their wits' end and would be only too glad to have me run it
for them again. I think all I'd have to do would be go and see
them and they'd offer me the position. Don't you think so,
Dick?' He said, 'Sure, they would, Jimmy. Only take my advice
and wait a while until business conditions are better. Then you
can strike them for a bigger salary than you got before, do you
see?' I said, 'Yes I do see, Dick, and many thanks for the tip.'
Well, conditions must be better by this time. All I have to do is
get fixed up with a decent front tomorrow, and it's as good as
done.

HOPE (*glances at* JIMMY *with a condescending affectionate pity – in a
hushed voice*). Poor Jimmy's off on his pipe dream again. Bejees,
he takes the cake!

This is too much for LARRY. *He cannot restrain a sardonic guffaw.
But no one pays any attention to him.*

LEWIS (*opens his eyes, which are drowsing again – dreamily to*
WETJOEN). I'm sorry we had to postpone our trip again this
April, Piet. I hoped the blasted old estate would be settled up
by then. The damned lawyers can't hold up the settlement
much longer. We'll make it next year, even if we have to work
and earn our passage money, eh? You'll stay with me at the old

place as long as you like, then you can take the *Union Castle* from Southampton to Cape Town. (*Sentimentally, with real yearning.*) England in April, I want you to see that, Piet. The old veldt has its points, I'll admit, but it isn't home – especially home in April.

WETJOEN (*blinks drowsily at him – dreamily*). Ja, Cecil, I know how beautiful it must be, from all you tell me many times. I vill enjoy it. But I shall enjoy more ven I am home, too. The veldt, ja! You could put England on it, and it would look like a farmer's small garden. Py Gott, there is space to be free, the air like vine is, you don't need booze to be drunk! My relations vill so surprised be. They vill not know me, it is so many years. Dey vill be so glad I haf come home at last.

JOE (*dreamily*). I'll make my stake and get my new gamblin' house open before you boys leave. You got to come to de openin'. I'll treat you white. If you're broke, I'll stake you to buck any game you chooses. If you wins, dat's velvet for you. If you loses, it don't count. Can't treat you no whiter dan dat, can I?

HOPE (*again with condescending pity*). Bejees, Jimmy's started them off smoking the same hop.

But the three are finished, their eyes closed again in sleep or a drowse.

LARRY (*aloud to himself – in his comically tense, crazy whisper*). Be God, this bughouse will drive me stark, raving loony yet!

HOPE (*turns on him with fuming suspicion*). What? What d'you say?

LARRY (*placatingly*). Nothing, Harry. I had a crazy thought in my head.

HOPE (*irascibly*). Crazy is right! Yah! The old wise guy! Wise hell! A damned old fool Anarchist I-Won't-Worker! I'm sick of you and Hugo, too. Bejees, you'll pay up tomorrow, or I'll start a Harry Hope Revolution! I'll tie a dispossess bomb to your tails that'll blow you out in the street! Bejees, I'll make your Movement move! (*The witticism delights him and he bursts into a shrill cackle.*)

At once MCGLOIN and MOSHER guffaw enthusiastically.

MOSHER (*flatteringly*). Harry, you sure say the funniest things! (*He reaches on the table as if he expected a glass to be there – then starts with well-acted surprise.*) Hell, where's my drink? That Rocky is too damned fast cleaning tables. Why, I'd only taken one sip of it.

HOPE (*his smiling face congealing*). No, you don't! (*Acidly.*) Any time you only take one sip of a drink, you'll have lockjaw and paralysis! Think you can kid me with those old circus con games? – me, that's known you since you was knee-high, and, bejees, you was a crook even then!

MCGLOIN (*grinning*). It's not like you to be so hard-hearted, Harry. Sure, it's hot, parching work laughing at your jokes so early in the morning on an empty stomach!

HOPE. Yah! You, Mac! Another crook! Who asked you to laugh? We was talking about poor old Bessie, and you and her no-good brother start to laugh! A hell of a thing! Talking mush about her, too! 'Good old Bess.' Bejees, she'd never forgive me if she knew I had you two bums living in her flat, throwing ashes and cigar butts on her carpet. You know her opinion of you, Mac. 'That Pat McGloin is the biggest drunken grafter that ever disgraced the police force,' she used to say to me. 'I hope they send him to Sing Sing for life.'

MCGLOIN (*unperturbed*). She didn't mean it. She was angry at me because you used to get me drunk. But Bess had a heart of gold underneath her sharpness. She knew I was innocent of all the charges.

WILLIE (*jumps to his feet drunkenly and points a finger at MCGLOIN – imitating the manner of a cross-examiner – coldly*). One moment, please. Lieutenant McGloin! Are you aware you are under oath? Do you realize what the penalty for perjury is? (*Purringly.*) Come now, Lieutenant, isn't it a fact that you're as guilty as hell? No, don't say, 'How about your old man?' I am asking the questions. The fact that he was a crooked old bucket-shop bastard has no bearing on your case. (*With a change to maudlin joviality.*) Gentlemen of the Jury, court will now recess while the DA sings out a little ditty he learned at Harvard. It was composed in a wanton moment by the Dean of the Divinity School on a moonlight night in July, 1776, while sobering up in a Turkish bath. (*He sings.*)

Oh, come up,' she cried, 'my sailor lad,
And you and I'll agree.
And I'll show you the prettiest (*Rap, rap, rap on table.*)
That ever you did see.'

Suddenly he catches HOPE's *eyes fixed on him condemningly, and sees* ROCKY *appearing from the bar. He collapses back on his chair, pleading miserably.*

Please, Harry! I'll be quiet! Don't make Rocky bounce me upstairs! I'll go crazy alone! (*To* MCGLOIN.) I apologize, Mac.

Don't get sore. I was only kidding you.

ROCKY, *at a relenting glance from* HOPE, *returns to the bar.*

MCGLOIN (*good-naturedly*). Sure, kid all you like, Willie. I'm
hardened to it. (*He pauses – seriously.*) But I'm telling you some
day before long I'm going to make them reopen my case.
Everyone knows there was no real evidence against me, and I
took the fall for the ones higher up. I'll be found innocent this
time and reinstated. (*Wistfully.*) I'd like to have my old job on
the Force back. The boys tell me there's fine pickings these
days, and I'm not getting rich here, sitting with a parched
throat waiting for Harry Hope to buy a drink. (*He glances
reproachfully at* HOPE.)

WILLIE. Of course, you'll be reinstated, Mac. All you need is a
brilliant young attorney to handle your case. I'll be straightened
out and on the wagon in a day or two. I've never practised but
I was one of the most brilliant students in Law School, and
your case is just the opportunity I need to start. (*Darkly.*) Don't
worry about my not forcing the DA to reopen your case. I went
through my father's papers before the cops destroyed them
and I remember a lot of people, even if I can't prove –
(*Coaxingly.*) You will let me take your case, won't you, Mac?

MCGLOIN (*soothingly*). Sure I will and it'll make your reputation,
Willie.

MOSHER *winks at* HOPE, *shaking his head, and* HOPE *answers
with identical pantomime, as though to say, 'Poor dopes, they're off
again!'*

LARRY (*aloud to himself more than to* PARRITT – *with irritable
wonder*). Ah, be damned! Haven't I heard their visions a
thousand times? Why should they get under my skin now? I've
got the blues, I guess. I wish to hell Hickey'd turn up.

MOSHER (*calculatingly solicitous – whispering to* HOPE). Poor
Willie needs a drink bad, Harry – and I think if we all joined
him it'd make him feel he was among friends and cheer him
up.

HOPE. More circus con tricks! (*Scathingly.*) You talking of your
dear sister! Bessie had you sized up. She used to tell me, 'I
don't know what you can see in that worthless, drunken, petty-
larceny brother of mine. If I had my way,' she'd say, 'he'd get
booted out in the gutter on his fat behind.' Sometimes she
didn't say behind, either.

MOSHER (*grins genially*). Yes, dear old Bess had a quick temper, but there was no real harm in her. (*He chuckles reminiscently,*) Remember the time she sent me down to the bar to change a ten-dollar bill for her?

HOPE (*has to grin himself*). Bejees, do I! She coulda bit a piece out of a stove lid, after she found it out. (*He cackles appreciatively.*)

MOSHER. I was sure surprised when she gave me the ten spot. Bess usually had better sense, but she was in a hurry to go to church. I didn't really mean to do it, but you know how habit gets you. Besides, I still worked then, and the circus season was going to begin soon, and I needed a little practice to keep my hand in. Or, you never can tell, the first rube that came to my wagon for a ticket might have left with the right change and I'd be disgraced. (*He chuckles.*) I said, 'I'm sorry, Bess, but I had to take it all in dimes. Here, hold out your hands and I'll count it out for you, so you won't kick afterwards I short-changed you.' (*He begins a count which grows more rapid as he goes on.*) Ten, twenty, thirty, forty, fifty, sixty, seventy, eighty, ninety, a dollar. Ten, twenty, thirty, forty, fifty, sixty – You're counting with me, Bess, aren't you? – eighty, ninety, two dollars. Ten, twenty – Those are pretty shoes you got on, Bess – forty, fifty, seventy, eighty, ninety, three dollars. Ten, twenty, thirty – What's on at the church tonight, Bess? – fifty, sixty, seventy, ninety, four dollars. Ten, twenty, thirty, fifty, seventy, eighty, ninety – That's a swell new hat, Bess, looks very becoming – six dollars. (*He chuckles.*) And so on. I'm bum at it now for lack of practice, but in those days I could have short-changed the Keeper of the Mint.

HOPE (*grinning*). Stung her for two dollars and a half, wasn't it, Ed?

MOSHER. Yes. A fine percentage, if I do say so, when you're dealing to someone who's sober and can count. I'm sorry to say she discovered my mistakes in arithmetic, just after I beat it around the corner. She counted it over herself. Bess somehow never had the confidence in me a sister should. (*He sighs tenderly.*) Dear Old Bess.

HOPE (*indignant now*). You're a fine guy bragging how you short-changed your own sister! Beejees, if there was a war and you was in it, they'd have to padlock the pockets of the dead!

MOSHER (*a bit hurt at this*). That's going pretty strong, Harry. I always gave a sucker some chance. There wouldn't be no fun robbing the dead. (*He becomes reminiscently melancholy.*) Gosh, thinking of the old ticket wagon brings those days back. The greatest life on earth with the greatest show on earth! The grandest crowd of regular guys ever gathered under one tent! I'd sure like to shake their hands again!

HOPE _(acidly)_. They'd have guns in theirs. They'd shoot you on sight. You've touched every damned one of them. Bejees, you've even borrowed fish from the seals and peanuts from every elephant that remembered you! (*This fancy tickles him and he gives a cackling laugh.*)

MOSHER (*overlooking this – dreamily*). You know, Harry, I've made up my mind I'll see the boss in a couple of days and ask for my old job. I can get back my magic touch with change easy, and I can throw him a line of bull that'll kid him I won't be so unreasonable about sharing the profits next time. (*With insinuating complaint.*) There's no percentage in hanging around this dive, taking care of you and shooting away your snakes, when I don't even get an eye-opener for my trouble.

HOPE (*implacably*). No!

MOSHER *sighs and gives up and closes his eyes. The others, except* LARRY *and* PARRITT, *are all dozing again now.* HOPE *goes on grumbling.*

Go to hell or the circus, for all I care. Good riddance bejees! I'm sick of you! (*Then worriedly.*) Say, Ed what the hell you think's happened to Hickey? I hope he'll turn up. Always got a million funny stories. You and the other bums have begun to give me the graveyard fantods. I'd like a good laugh with old Hickey. (*He chuckles at a memory.*) Remember that gag he always pulls about his wife and the iceman? He'd make a cat laugh!

ROCKY *appears from the bar. He comes front, behind* MOSHER's *chair, and begins pushing the black curtain along the rod to the rear wall.*

ROCKY. Openin' time, Boss. (*He presses a button at rear which switches off the lights. The back room becomes drabber and dingier than ever in the grey daylight that comes from the street windows, off right, and what light can penetrate the grime of the two backyard windows at left.* ROCKY *turns back to* HOPE *– grumpily.*) Why don't you go up to bed, Boss? Hickey'd never turn up dis time of de mornin'!

HOPE (*starts and listens*). Someone's coming now.

ROCKY (*listens*). Aw, dat's on'y my two pigs. It's about time dey showed. (*He goes back towards the door of the bar.*)

HOPE (*sourly disappointed*). You keep them dumb broads quiet. I don't want to go to bed. I'm going to catch a couple more winks here and I don't want no damn-fool laughing and screeching. (*He settles himself in his chair, grumbling.*) Never thought I'd see the day when Harry Hope's would have tarts rooming in it. What'd Bessie think? But I don't let 'em use my rooms for business. And they're good kids. Good as anyone else. They got to make a living. Pay their rent, too, which is more than I can say for – (*He cocks an eye over his specs at* MOSHER *and grins with satisfaction.*) Bejees, Ed, I'll bet Bessie is doing somersaults in her grave! (*He chuckles.*)

But MOSHER's *eyes are closed, his head nodding, and he doesn't reply, so* HOPE *closes his eyes.* ROCKY *has opened the bar-room door at rear and is standing in the hall beyond it, facing right. A girl's laugh is heard.*

ROCKY (*warningly*). Nix! Piano!

He comes in, beckoning them to follow. He goes behind the bar and gets a whisky bottle and glasses and chairs. MARGIE *and* PEARL *follow him, casting a glance around. Everyone except* LARRY *and* PARRITT *is asleep or dozing. Even* PARRITT *has his eyes closed. The two girls, neither much over twenty, are typically dollar street-walkers, dressed in the usual tawdry get-up.* PEARL *is obviously Italian with black hair and eyes.* MARGIE *has brown hair and hazel eyes, a slum New Yorker of mixed blood. Both are plump and have a certain prettiness that shows even through their blobby make-up. Each retains a vestige of youthful freshness, although the game is beginning to get them and give them hard, worn expressions. Both are sentimental, feather-brained, giggly, lazy, good-natured and reasonably contented with life. Their attitude towards* ROCKY *is much that of two maternal affectionate sisters toward a bullying brother whom they like to tease and spoil. His attitude towards them is that of the owner of two performing pets he has trained to do a profitable act under his management. He feels a proud proprietor's affection for them, and is tolerantly lax in his discipline.*

MARGIE (*glancing around*). Jees, Poil, it's de Morgue wid all de stiffs on deck. (*She catches* LARRY's *eye and smiles affectionately.*) Hello, Old Wise Guy, ain't you died yet?

LARRY (*grinning*). Not yet, Margie. But I'm waiting impatiently for the end.

PARRITT *opens his eyes to look at the two girls, but as soon as they glance at him he closes them again and turns his head away.*

MARGIE (*as she and* PEARL *come to the table at right, front, followed by* ROCKY). Who's de new guy? Friend of yours, Larry? (*Automatically she smiles seductively and addresses him in a professional chant.*) Wanta have a good time, kid?

PEARL. Aw, he's passed out. Hell wid him!

HOPE (*cocks an eye over his specs at them – with drowsy irritation*). You dumb broads cut the loud talk. (*He shuts his eye again.*)

ROCKY (*admonishing them good-naturedly*). Sit down before I knock yuh down.

MARGIE *and* PEARL *sit at left, and rear, of table,* ROCKY *at right of it. The girls pour drinks.* ROCKY *begins in a brisk, businesslike manner but in a lowered voice with an eye on* HOPE.

Well, how'd you tramps do?

MARGIE. Pretty Good. Didn't we, Poil?

PEARL. Sure. We nailed a coupla all-night guys.

MARGIE. On Sixth Avenoo. Boobs from de sticks.

PEARL. Stinko, de bot' of 'em.

MARGIE. We thought we was in luck. We steered dem to a real hotel. We figgered dey was too stinko to bother us much and we could cop a good sleep in beds that ain't got cobble stones in de mattress like de ones in dis dump.

PEARL. But we was outa luck. Dey didn't bother us much dat way, but dey wouldn't go to sleep either see? Jees, I never hoid such gabby guys.

MARGIE. Dey got onta politics, drinkin' outa de bottle. Dey forgot we was around. 'De Bull Moosen is de on'y reg'lar guys,' one guy says. And de other guy says. 'You're a God-damned liar! And I'm a Republican!' Den dey'd laugh.

PEARL. Den dey'd get mad and make a bluff dey was goin' to scrap, and den dey'd make up and cry and sing 'School Days'. Jees, imagine tryin' to sleep wid dat on de phonograph!

MARGIE. Maybe you tink we wasn't glad when de house dick come up and told us all to git dressed and take de air!

PEARL. We told de guys we'd wait for dem 'round de corner.

MARGIE. So here we are.

ROCKY (*sententiously*). Yeah. I see you. But I don't see no dough yet.

PEARL (*with a wink at* MARGIE – *teasingly*). Right on de job, ain't he, Margie?

MARGIE. Yeah, our little business man! Dat's him!

ROCKY. Come on! Dig!

They both pull up their skirts to get the money from their stockings. ROCKY watches this move carefully.

PEARL (*amused*). Pipe him keepin' cases, Margie.

MARGIE (*amused*). Scared we're holdin' out on him.

PEARL. Way he grabs, yuh'd tink it was him done de woik. (*She holds out a little roll of bills to* ROCKY.) Here y'are, Grafter!

MARGIE (*holding hers out*). We hope it chokes yuh.

ROCKY counts the money quickly and shoves it in his pocket.

ROCKY (*genially*). You dumb baby dolls gimme a pain. What would you do wid money if I wasn't around? Give it all to some pimp.

PEARL (*teasingly*). Jees, what's the difference –? (*Hastily.*) Aw, I don't mean dat, Rocky.

ROCKY (*his eyes growing hard – slowly*). A lotta difference, get me?

PEARL. Don't get sore. Jees, can't yuh take a little kiddin'?

MARGIE. Sure, Rocky, Poil was on'y kiddin'. (*Soothingly.*) We know yuh got a reg'lar job. Dat's why we like yuh, see? Yuh don't live offa us. Yuh're a bartender.

ROCKY (*genially again*). Sure, I'm a bartender. Everyone knows me knows dat. And I treat you goils right, don't I? Jees, I'm wise yuh hold out on me, but I know it ain't much, so what the hell, I let yuh get away wid it. I tink yuh're a coupla good kids. Yuh're aces wid me, see?

PEARL. You're aces wid us, too. Ain't he, Margie?

MARGIE. Sure, he's aces.

ROCKY beams complacently and takes the glasses back to the bar. MARGIE whispers.

Yuh sap, don't yuh know enough not to kid him on dat? Serve yuh right if he beat yuh up!

PEARL (*admiringly*). Jees, I'll bet he'd give yuh an awful beatin', too, once he started. Ginnies got awful tempers.

MARGIE. Anyway, we wouldn't keep no pimp, like we was reg'lar old whores. We ain't dat bad.

PEARL. No. We're tarts, but dat's all.

ROCKY (*rinsing glasses behind the bar*). Cora got back around three o'clock. She woke up Chuck and dragged him outa de hay to go to a chop suey joint. (*Disgustedly.*) Imagine him standin' for dat stuff!

MARGIE (*disgustedly*). I'll bet dey been sittin' around kiddin' demselves wid dat old pipe dream about gettin' married and settlin' down on a farm. Jees, when Chuck's on de wagon, dey never lay off dat dope! Dey give yuh an earful every time yuh talk to 'em!

PEARL. Yeah. Chuck wid a willy grin on his ugly map, de big boob, and Cora gigglin' like she was in grammar school and some tough guy'd just told her babies wasn't brung down de chimney by a boid!

MARGIE. And her on de turf long before me and you was! And bot' of em' arguin' all de time, Cora sayin' she's scared to marry him because he'll go on drunks again. Just as dough any drunk could scare Cora!

PEARL. And him swearin', de big liar, he'll never go on no more periodicals! An' den her pretendin' – But it gives me a pain to talk about it. We ought to phone de booby hatch to send round de wagon for 'em.

ROCKY (*comes back to the table – disgustedly*). Yeah, of all de pipe dreams in dis dump dey got de nuttiest! And nuttin' stops dem. Dey been dreamin' it for years, every time Chuck goes on de wagon. I never could figger it. What would gettin' married get dem? But de farm stuff is de sappiest part. When bot' of 'em was dragged up in dis ward and ain't never been nearer a farm dan Coney Island! Jees, dey'd tink dey'd gone deef if dey didn't hear de El rattle! Dey'd get DT's if dey ever hoid a cricket choip! I hoid crickets once on my cousin's place in Joisey. I couldn't sleep a wink. Dey give me de heebie-jeebies. (*With deeper disgust.*) Jees, can yuh picture a good barkeep like Chuck diggin' spuds? And imagine a whore hustlin' de cows home! For Christ safe! Ain't dat a sweet picture!

MARGIE (*rebukingly*). Yuh oughtn't to call Cora dat, Rocky. She's a good kid. She may be a tart, but –

ROCKY (*considerately*). Sure, dat's all I meant, a tart.

PEARL (*giggling*). But he's right about de damned cows, Margie. Jees, I bet Cora don't know which end of de cow has de horns! I'm goin' to ask her.

There is the noise of a door opening in the hall and the sound of a man's and woman's arguing voices.

ROCKY. Here's your chance. Dat's dem two nuts now.

CORA *and* CHUCK *look in from the hallway and then come in.* CORA *is a thin peroxide blonde, a few years older than* PEARL *and* MARGIE, *dressed in similar style, her round-face showing more of the wear and tear of her trade than theirs, but still with traces of a doll-like prettiness.* CHUCK *is a tough, thick-necked, barrel-chested Italian-American, with a fat, amiable, swarthy face. He has on a straw hat with a vivid band, a loud suit, tie and shirt, and yellow shoes. His eyes are clear and he looks healthy and strong as an ox.*

CORA (*gaily*). Hello, bums. (*She looks around.*) Jees, de Morgue on a rainy Sunday night! (*She waves to* LARRY – *affectionately.*) Hello, Old Wise Guy! Ain't you croaked yet?

LARRY (*grins.*) Not yet, Cora. It's damned tiring, this waiting for the end.

CORA. Aw, gwan, you'll never die! Yuh'll have to hire someone to croak yuh wid an axe.

HOPE (*cocks one sleepy eye at her – irritably*). You dumb hookers, cut the loud noise! This ain't a cat-house!

CORA (*teasingly*). My, Harry! Such language!

HOPE (*closes his eyes – to himself with a gratified chuckle*). Bejees, I'll bet Bessie's turning over in her grave!

CORA *sits down between* MARGIE *and* PEARL, CHUCK *takes an empty chair from* HOPE's *table and puts it by hers and sits down. At* LARRY's *table,* PARRITT *is glaring resentfully towards the girls.*

PARRITT. If I'd known this dump was a hooker hangout, I'd never have come here.

LARRY (*watching him*). You seem down on the ladies.

PARRITT (*vindictively*). I hate every bitch that ever lived! They're all alike! (*Catching himself guiltily.*) You can understand how I feel, can't you, when it was getting mixed up with a tart that made me have that fight with Mother? (*Then with a resentful sneer.*) But what the hell does it matter to you? You're in the grandstand. You're through with life.

LARRY (*sharply*). I'm glad you remember it. I don't want to know a damned thing about your business. (*He closes his eyes and settles on his chair as if preparing for sleep.*)

PARRITT *stares at him sneeringly. Then he looks away and his expression becomes furtive and frightened.*

CORA. Who's de guy wid Larry?

ROCKY. A tightwad. To hell wid him.

PEARL. Say, Cora, wise me up. Which end of a cow is de horns on?

CORA (*embarrassed*). Aw, don't bring dat up. I'm sick of hearin' about dat farm.

ROCKY. You got nuttin' on us!

CORA (*ignoring this*). Me and dis overgrown tramp has been scrappin' about it. He says Joisey's de best place, and I says Long Island because we'll be near Coney. And I tells him, How do I know yuh're off of periodicals for life? I don't give a damn how drunk yuh get, the way we are, but I don't wanta be married to no soak.

CHUCK. And I tells her I'm off de stuff for life. Den she beefs we won't be married a month before I'll trow it in her face she was a tart. 'Jees, Baby,' I tells her. 'Why should I? What de hell yuh tink I tink I'm marryin', a voigin? Why should I kick as long as yuh lay off it and don't do no cheatin' wid de iceman or nobody?' (*He gives her a rough hug.*) Dat's on de level, Baby. (*He kisses her.*)

CORA (*kissing him*). Aw, yuh big tramp!

ROCKY (*shakes his head with profound disgust*). Can yuh tie it? I'll buy a drink. I'll do anything. (*He gets up.*)

CORA. No, dis round's on me. I run into luck. Dat's why I dragged Chuck outa bed to celebrate. It was a sailor. I rolled him. (*She giggles.*) Listen, it was a scream. I've run into some nutty souses, but dis guy was de nuttiest. De booze dey dish out around de Brooklyn Navy Yard must be as turrible bugjuice as Harry's. My dogs was givin' out when I seen dis guy holdin' up a lamp-post, so I hurried to get him before a cop did. I says, 'Hello, Handsome, wanta have a good time?' Jees, he was paralysed! One of dem polite jags. He tries to bow to me, imagine, and I had to prop him up or he'd fell on his nose. And what d'yuh tink he said? 'Lady', he says, 'can yuh kindly tell me de nearest way to de Museum of Natural History?' (*They all laugh.*) Can yuh imagine! At two a.m. As if I'd know where de dump was anyway. But I says, 'Sure ting, Honey Boy, I'll be only too glad.' So I steered him into a side street where it was dark and propped him against a wall and give him a frisk. (*She giggles.*) And what d'yuh tink he does? Jees, I ain't lyin', he begins to laugh, de big sap! He says, 'Quit ticklin' me.' While I was friskin' him for his roll! I near died! Den I toined him 'round and give him a push to start him. 'Just keep goin',' I told him. 'It's a big white building on your right. You can't miss it.' He must be swimmin' in de North River yet!

They all laugh.

CHUCK. Ain't Uncle Sam de sap to trust guys like dat wid dough!

CORA (*with a businesslike air*). I picked twelve bucks offa him. Come on, Rocky. Set 'em up.

ROCKY *goes back to the bar.* CORA *looks around the room.*

Say, Chuck's kiddin' about de iceman a minute ago reminds me. Where de hell's Hickey?

ROCKY. Dat's what we're all wonderin'.

CORA. He oughta be here. Me and Chuck seen him.

ROCKY (*excited, comes back from the bar, forgetting the drinks*). You seen Hickey? (*He nudges* HOPE.) Hey, Boss, come to! Cora's seen Hickey.

HOPE *is instantly wide awake and everyone in the place except* HUGO *and* PARRITT, *begins to rouse up hopefully, as if a mysterious wireless message had gone round.*

HOPE. Where'd you see him, Cora?

CORA. Right on de next corner. He was standin' dere. We said, 'Welcome to our city. De gang is expectin' yuh wid deir tongues hangin' out a yard long.' And I kidded him, 'How's de iceman, Hickey? How's he doin' at your house?' He laughs and says, 'Fine.' And he says, 'Tell de gang I'll be along in a minute. I'm just finishin' figurin' out de best way to save dem and bring dem peace.'

HOPE (*chuckles*). Bejees, he's thought up a new gag! It's a wonder he didn't borry a Salvation Army uniform and show up in that! Go out and get him, Rocky. Tell him we're waitin' to be saved!

ROCKY *goes out, grinning.*

CORA. Yeah, Harry, he was only kiddin'. But he was funny, too, somehow. He was different, or somethin'.

CHUCK. Sure, he was sober, Baby. Dat's what made him different. We ain't never seen him when he wasn't on a drunk, or had de willies gettin' over it.

CORA. Sure! Gee, ain't I dumb?

HOPE (*with conviction*). The dumbest broad I ever seen! (*Then puzzledly.*) Sober? That's funny. He's always lapped up a good starter on his way here. Well, bejees, he won't be sober long! He'll be good and ripe for my birthday party tonight at twelve. (*He chuckles with excited anticipation – addressing all of them.*) Listen! He's fixed some new gag to pull on us. We'll pretend to let him kid us, see? And we'll kid the pants off him.

They all say laughingly, 'Sure, Harry,' 'Righto,' 'That's the stuff,' 'We'll fix him,' *etc., etc., their faces excited with the same eager anticipation.* ROCKY *appears in the doorway at the end of the bar with* HICKY, *his arm around* HICKY's *shoulders.*

ROCKY (*with an affectionate grin*). Here's the old son of a bitch!

They all stand up and greet him with affectionate acclaim, 'Hello, Hickey' *etc. Even* HUGO *comes out of his coma to raise his head and blink through his thick spectacles with a welcoming giggle.*

HICKEY (*jovially*). Hello, Gang! (*He stands a moment, beaming around at all of them affectionately. He is about fifty, a little under medium height, with a stout, roly-poly figure. His face is round and smooth and big-boyish with bright blue eyes, a button nose, a small, pursed mouth. His head is bald except for a fringe of hair around his temples and the back of his head. His expression is fixed in a salesman's winning smile of self-confident affability and hearty good fellowship. His eyes have the twinkle of a humour which delights in kidding others but can also enjoy equally a joke on himself. He exudes a friendly, generous personality that makes everyone like him on sight. You get the impression, too, that he must have real ability in his line. There is an efficient, businesslike approach in his manner, and his eyes can take you in shrewdly at a glance. He has the salesman's mannerisms of speech, an easy flow of glib, persuasive convincingness. His clothes are those of a successful drummer whose territory consists of minor cities and small towns – not flashy but conspicuously spic and span. He immediately puts on an entrance act, places a hand affectedly on his chest, throws back his head, and sings in a falsetto tenor.*) 'It's always fair weather, when good fellows get together!' (*Changing to a comic bass and another tune.*) 'And another little drink won't do us any harm!' (*They all roar with laughter at this burlesque which his*

*personality makes really funny. He waves his hand in a lordly manner
to* ROCKY.) Do your duty, Brother Rocky. Bring on the rat
poison!

ROCKY *grins and goes behind the bar to get drinks amid an
approving cheer from the crowd.* HICKEY *comes forward to shake
hands with* HOPE – *with affectionate heartiness.*

How goes it, Governor?

HOPE (*enthusiastically*). Bejees, Hickey, you old bastard, it's good
to see you!

HICKEY *shakes hands with* MOSHER *and* MCGLOIN; *leans right
to shake hands with* MARGIE *and* PEARL; *moves to the middle table
to shake hands with* LEWIS, JOE MOTT, WETJOEN *and*
JIMMY; *waves to* WILLIE, LARRY *and* HUGO. *He greets each by
name with the same affectionate heartiness and there is an interchange
of* 'How's the kid?' 'How's the old scout?' 'How's the boy?'
'How's everything?' *etc., etc.* ROCKY *begins setting out drinks,
whisky glasses with chasers, and a bottle for each table, starting with*
LARRY's *table.* HOPE *says.*

Sit down, Hickey. Sit down.

HICKEY *takes the chair, facing front, at the front of the table in the
second row which is half between* HOPE's *table and the one where*
JIMMY TOMORROW *is.* HOPE *goes on with excited pleasure.*

Bejees, Hickey, it seems natural to see your ugly, grinning map.
(*With a scornful nod to* CORA.) This dumb broad was tryin' to
tell us you'd changed, but you ain't a damned bit. Tell us about
yourself. How've you been doin'? Bejees, you look like a million
dollars.

ROCKY (*coming to* HICKEY's *table, puts a bottle of whisky, a glass
and a chaser on it – then hands.* HICKEY *a key*). Here's your key,
Hickey. Same old room.

HICKEY (*shoves the key in his pocket*). Thanks, Rocky. I'm going up
in a little while and grab a snooze. Haven't been able to sleep
lately and I'm tired as hell. A couple of hours good kip will fix
me.

HOPE (*as* ROCKY *puts drinks on his table*). First time I ever heard
you worry about sleep. Bejees, you never would go to bed.

He raises his glass, and all the others except PARRITT *do likewise.*

Get a few slugs under your belt and you'll forget sleeping.
Here's mud in your eye, Hickey.

They all join in with the usual humorous toasts.

HICKEY (*heartily*). Drink hearty, boys and girls!

They all drink, but HICKEY *drinks only his chaser.*

HOPE. Bejees, is that a new stunt, drinking your chaser first?

HICKEY. No, I forgot to tell Rocky – You'll have to excuse me, boys and girls, but I'm off the stuff. For keeps.

They stare at him in amazed incredulity.

HOPE. What the hell – (*Then with a wink at the others, kiddingly.*) Sure! Joined the Salvation Army, ain't you? Been elected President of the WCTU? Take that bottle away from him, Rocky. We don't want to tempt him into sin. (*He chuckles and the others laugh.*)

HICKEY (*earnestly*). No, honest, Harry. I know it's hard to believe but – (*He pauses – then adds simply.*) Cora was right, Harry. I have changed. I mean, about booze. I don't need it any more.

They all stare, hoping it's a gag, but impressed and disappointed and made vaguely uneasy by the change they now sense in him.

HOPE (*his kidding a bit forced*). Yeah, go ahead, kid the pants off us! Bejees, Cora said you was coming to save us! Well, go on. Get this joke off your chest! Start the service! Sing a God-damned hymn if you like. We'll all join in the chorus. 'No drunkard can enter this beautiful home.' That's a good one. (*He forces a cackle.*)

HICKEY (*grinning*). Oh, hell, Governor! You don't think I'd come around here peddling some brand of temperance bunk, do you? You know me better than that! Just because I'm through with the stuff don't mean I'm going Prohibition. Hell, I'm not that ungrateful! It's given me too many good times. I feel exactly the same as I always did. If anyone wants to get drunk, if that's the only way they can be happy, and feel at peace with themselves, why the hell shouldn't they? They have my full and entire sympathy. I know all about that game from soup to nuts. I'm the guy that wrote the book. The only reason I've quit is – Well, I finally had the guts to face myself and throw overboard the damned lying pipe dream that'd been making me miserable, and do what I had to do for the happiness of all concerned – and then all at once I found I was at peace with myself and I didn't need booze any more. That's all there was to it. (*He pauses. They are staring at him, uneasy and*

beginning to feel defensive. HICKEY *looks round and grins*
affectionately – apologetically.) But what the hell! Don't let me be
a wet blanket, making fool speeches about myself. Set 'em up
again, Rocky. Here. (*He pulls a big roll from his pocket and peels off*
a ten-dollar bill. The faces of all brighten.) Keep the balls coming
until this is killed. Then ask for more.

ROCKY. Jees, a roll dat'd choke a hippopotamus! Fill up, youse
guys.

They all pour out drinks.

HOPE. That sounds more like you, Hickey. That water-wagon
bull – Cut out the act and have a drink, for Christ's sake.

HICKEY. It's no act, Governor. But don't get me wrong. That
don't mean I'm a teetotal grouch and can't be in the party.
Hell, why d'you suppose I'm here except to have a party, same
as I've always done and help celebrate your birthday tonight?
You've all been good pals to me, the best friends I've ever had.
I've been thinking about you ever since I left the house – all
the time I was walking over here –

HOPE. Walking? Bejees, do you mean to say you walked?

HICKEY. I sure did. All the way from the wilds of darkest
Astoria. Didn't mind it a bit, either. I seemed to get here before
I knew it. I'm a bit tired and sleepy but otherwise I feel great.
(*Kiddingly.*) That ought to encourage you, Governor – show you
a little walk around the ward is nothing to be so scared about.
(*He winks at the others.* HOPE *stiffens resentfully for a second.*
HICKEY *goes on.*) I didn't make such bad time either for a fat
guy, considering it's a hell of a ways, and I sat in the park a
while thinking. It was going on twelve when I went in the
bedroom to tell Evelyn I was leaving. Six hours, say. No, less
than that. I'd been standing on the corner some time before
Cora and Chuck came along, thinking about all of you. Of
course, I was only kidding Cora with that stuff about saving
you. (*Then seriously.*) No, I wasn't either. But I didn't mean
booze. I meant save you from pipe dreams. I know now, from
my experience, they're the things that really poison and ruin a
guy's life and keep him from finding any peace. If you knew
how free and contented I feel now. I'm like a new man. And
the cure for them is so damned simple, once you have the
nerve. Just the old dope of honesty is the best policy – honesty
with yourself, I mean. Just stop lying about yourself and
kidding yourself about tomorrows. (*He is staring ahead of him*

now as if he were talking aloud to himself as much as to them. Their eyes are fixed on him with uneasy resentment. His manner becomes apologetic again.) Hell, this begins to sound like a damned sermon on the way to lead the good life. Forget that part of it. It's in my blood, I guess. My old man used to whale salvation into my heinie with a birch rod. He was a preacher in the sticks of Indiana, like I've told you. I got my knack of sales gab from him, too. He was the boy who could sell those Hoosier hayseeds building lots along the Golden Street! (*Taking on a salesman's persuasiveness.*) Now listen, boys and girls, don't look at me as if I was trying to sell you a goldbrick. Nothing up my sleeve, honest. Let's take an example. Any one of you. Take you, Governor. That walk around the ward you never take –

HOPE (*defensively sharp*). What about it?

HICKEY (*grinning affectionately*). Why, you know as well as I do, Harry. Everything about it.

HOPE (*defiantly*). Bejees, I'm going to take it!

HICKEY. Sure, you're going to – this time. Because I'm going to help you. I know it's the thing you've got to do before you'll ever know what real peace means. (*He looks at* JIMMY TOMORROW.) Same thing with you, Jimmy. You've got to try and get your old job back. And no tomorrow about it! (*As* JIMMY *stiffens with a pathetic attempt at dignity – placatingly.*) No, don't tell me, Jimmy. I know all about tomorrow. I'm the guy that wrote the book.

JIMMY. I don't understand you. I admit I've foolishly delayed, but as it happens, I'd just made up my mind that as soon as I could get straightened out –

HICKEY. Fine! That's the spirit! And I'm going to help you. You've been damned kind to me, Jimmy, and I want to prove how grateful I am. When it's all over and you don't have to nag at yourself any more, you'll be grateful to me, too! (*He looks around at the others.*) And all the rest of you, ladies included, are in the same boat, one way or another.

LARRY (*who has been listening with sardonic appreciation – in his comically intense, crazy whisper*). Be God, you've hit the nail on the head, Hickey! This dump is the Palace of Pipe Dreams!

HICKEY (*grins at him with affectionate kidding*). Well, well! The Old Grandstand Foolosopher speaks! You think you're the big exception, eh? Life doesn't mean a damn to you any more, does it? You're retired from the circus. You're just waiting impatiently for the end – the good old Long Sleep! (*He chuckles.*) Well, I think a lot of you, Larry, you old bastard. I'll try and make an honest man of you, too!

LARRY (*stung*). What the devil are you hinting at, anyway?

HICKEY. You don't have to ask me, do you, a wise old guy like you? Just ask yourself. I'll bet you know.

PARRITT (*is watching LARRY's face with a curious sneering satisfaction*). He's got your number all right, Larry! (*He turns to HICKEY.*) That's the stuff, Hickey. Show the old faker up! He's got no right to sneak out of everything.

HICKEY (*regards him with surprise at first, then with a puzzled interest*). Hello. A stranger in our midst. I didn't notice you before, Brother.

PARRITT (*embarrassed, his eyes shifting away*). My name's Parritt. I'm an old friend of Larry's. (*His eyes come back to HICKEY to find him still sizing him up – defensively.*) Well? What are you staring at?

HICKEY (*continuing to stare – puzzledly*). No offence, Brother. I was trying to figure – Haven't we met before some place?

PARRITT (*reassured*). No. First time I've ever been East.

HICKEY. No, you're right. I know that's not it. In my game, to be a shark at it, you teach yourself never to forget a name or a face. But still I know damned well I recognized something about you. We're members of the same lodge – in some way.

PARRITT (*uneasy again*). What are you talking about? You're nuts.

HICKEY (*dryly*). Don't try to kid me, Little Boy. I'm a good salesman – so damned good the firm was glad to take me back after every drunk – and what made me good was I could size up anyone. (*Frowningly puzzled again.*) But I don't see – (*Suddenly breezily good-natured.*) Never mind. I can tell you're having trouble with yourself and I'll be glad to do anything I can to help a friend of Larry's.

LARRY. Mind your own business, Hickey. He's nothing to you – or to me, either. (HICKEY *gives him a keen inquisitive glance.* LARRY *looks away and goes on sarcastically.*) You're keeping us all in suspense. Tell us more about how you're going to save us.

HICKEY (*good-naturedly but seeming a little hurt*). Hell, don't get sore, Larry. Not at me. We've always been good pals, haven't we? I know I've always liked you a lot.

LARRY (*a bit shamefacedly*). Well, so have I liked you. Forget it, Hickey.

HICKEY (*beaming*). Fine! That's the spirit! (*Looking around at the others, who have forgotten their drinks.*) What's the matter, everybody? What is this, a funeral? Come on and drink up! A little action! (*They all drink.*) Have another. Hell, this is a celebration! Forget it, it anything I've said sounds too serious. I don't want to be a pain in the neck. Any time you think I'm talking out of turn, just tell me to go chase myself! (*He yawns with growing drowsiness and his voice grows a bit muffled.*) No, boys and girls, I'm not trying to put anything over on you. It's just that I know now from experience what a lying pipe dream can do to you – and how damned relieved and contented with yourself you feel when you're rid of it. (*He yawns again.*) God, I'm sleepy all of a sudden. That long walk is beginning to get me. I better go upstairs. Hell of a trick to go dead on you like this. (*He starts to get up but relaxes again. His eyes blink as he tries to keep them open.*) No, boys and girls, I've never known what real peace was until now. It's a grand feeling, like when you're sick and suffering like hell and the Doc gives you a shot in the arm, and the pain goes, and you drift off. (*His eyes close.*) You can let go of yourself at last. Let yourself sink down to the bottom of the sea. Rest in peace. There's no farther you have to go. Not a single damned hope or dream left to nag you. You'll all know what I mean after you – (*He pauses – mumbles.*) Excuse – all in – got to grab forty winks – Drink up, everybody – on me – (*The sleep of complete exhaustion overpowers him. His chin sags to his chest.*)

They stare at him with puzzled uneasy fascination.

HOPE (*forcing a tone of irritation*). Bejees, that's a fine stunt, to go to sleep on us! (*Then fumingly to the crowd.*) Well, what the hell's the matter with you bums? Why don't you drink up? You're always crying for booze, and now you've got it under your nose, you sit like dummies! (*They start and gulp down their whiskies and pour another. HOPE stares at HICKEY.*) Bejees, I can't figure Hickey. I still say he's kidding us. Kid his own grandmother, Hickey would. What d'you think, Jimmy?

JIMMY (*unconvincingly*). It must be another of his jokes, Harry, although – Well, he does appear changed. But he'll probably be his natural self again tomorrow – (*Hastily.*) I mean, when he wakes up.

LARRY (*staring at* HICKEY *frowningly – more aloud to himself than to them*). You'll make a mistake if you think he's only kidding.

PARRITT (*in a low confidential voice*). I don't like that guy, Larry. He's too damned nosy. I'm going to steer clear of him.

LARRY *gives him a suspicious glance, then looks hastily away.*

JIMMY (*with an attempt at open-minded reasonableness*). Still, Harry, I have to admit there was some sense in his nonsense. It is time I got my job back – although I hardly need him to remind me.

HOPE (*with an air of frankness*). Yes, and I ought to take a walk around the ward. But I don't need no Hickey to tell me, seeing I got it all set for my birthday tomorrow.

LARRY (*sardonically*). Ha! (*Then in his comically intense, crazy whisper.*) Be God, it looks like he's going to make two sales of his peace at least! But you'd better make sure first it's the real McCoy and not poison.

HOPE (*disturbed – angrily*). You bughouse I-Won't-Work harp, who asked you to shove in an oar? What the hell d'you mean, poison? Just because he has your number – (*He immediately feels ashamed of this taunt and adds apologetically.*) Bejees, Larry, you're always croaking about something to do with death. It gets my nanny. Come on, fellers, let's drink up. (*They drink.* HOPE's *eyes are fixed on* HICKEY *again.*) Stone cold sober and dead to the world! Spilling that business about pipe dreams! Bejees, I don't get it. (*He bursts out again in angry complaint.*) He ain't like the old Hickey! He'll be a fine wet blanket to have around at my birthday party! I wish to hell he'd never turned up!

MOSHER (*who has been the least impressed by* HICKEY's *talk and is the first to recover and feel the effect of the drinks on top of his hangover – genially*). Give him time, Harry, and he'll come out of it. I've watched many cases of almost fatal teetotalism, but they all came out of it completely cured and as drunk as ever. My opinion is the poor sap is temporarily bughouse from overwork. (*Musingly.*) You can't be too careful about work. It's the deadliest habit known to science, a great physician once told me. He practised on street corners under a torchlight. He was positively the only doctor in the world who claimed that rattlesnake oil, rubbed on the prat, would cure heart failure in three days. I remember well his saying to me, 'You are naturally delicate, Ed, but if you drink a pint of bad whisky before breakfast every evening, and never work if you can help it, you may live to a ripe old age. It's staying sober and working that cuts men off in their prime.'

While he is talking, they turn to him with eager grins. They are longing to laugh, and as he finishes they roar. Even PARRITT *laughs.* HICKEY *sleeps on like a dead man, but* HUGO, *who had passed into his customary coma again, head on table, looks up through his thick spectacles and giggles foolishly.*

HUGO (*blinking around at them. As the laughter dies he speaks in his giggling, wheedling manner, as if he were playfully teasing children*). Laugh, leedle bourgeois monkey-faces! Laugh like fools, leedle stupid peoples. (*His tone suddenly changes to one of guttural soapbox denunciation and he pounds on the table with a small fist.*) I vill laugh, too! But I vill laugh last! I vill laugh at you! (*He declaims his favourite quotation.*) 'The days grow hot, O Babylon! 'Tis cool beneath thy villow trees!'

They all hoot him down in a chorus of amused jeering. HUGO *is not offended. This is evidently their customary reaction. He giggles goodnaturedly.* HICKEY *sleeps on. They have all forgotten their uneasiness about him now and ignore him.*

LEWIS (*tipsily*). Well, now that our little Robespierre has got the daily bit of guillotining off his chest, tell me more about your doctor friend, Ed. He strikes me as the only bloody sensible medico I ever heard of. I think we should appoint him house physician here without a moment's delay.

They all laughingly assent.

MOSHER (*warming to his subject, shakes his head sadly*). Too late! The old Doc has passed on to his Maker. A victim of overwork, too. He didn't follow his own advice. Kept his nose to the grindstone and sold one bottle of snake oil too many. Only eighty years old when he was taken. The saddest part was that he knew he was doomed. The last time we got paralysed together he told me: 'This game will get me yet, Ed. You see before you a broken man, a martyr to medical science. If I had any nerves I'd have a nervous breakdown. You won't believe me, but this last year there was actually one night I had so many patients, I didn't even have time to get drunk. The shock to my system brought on a stroke which, as a doctor, I recognized was the beginning of the end.' Poor old Doc! When he said this he started crying. 'I hate to go before my task is completed, Ed,' he sobbed. 'I'd hoped I'd live to see the day when, thanks to my miraculous cure, there wouldn't be a single vacant cemetery lot left in this glorious country.' (*There is a roar of laughter. He waits for it to die and then goes on sadly.*) I miss Doc. He was a gentleman of the old school. I'll bet he's standing on a street corner in hell right now, making suckers of the damned, telling them there's nothing like snake oil for a bad burn.

There is another roar of laughter. This time it penetrates HICKEY's *exhausted slumber. He stirs on his chair, trying to wake up, managing to raise his head a little and force his eyes half open. He speaks with a drowsy, affectionately encouraging smile. At once the laughter stops abruptly and they turn to him startledly.*

HICKEY. That's the spirit – don't let me be a wet blanket – all I want is to see you happy – (*He slips back into heavy sleep again.*)

They all stare at him, their faces again puzzled, resentful and uneasy.

Curtain.

ACT TWO

Scene. The back room only. The black curtain dividing it from the bar is the right wall of the scene. It is getting on towards midnight of the same day.

The back room has been prepared for a festivity. At centre, front, four of the circular tables are pushed together to form one long table with an uneven line of chairs behind it, and chairs at each end. This improvised banquet table is covered with old table-cloths, borrowed from a neighbouring beanery, and is laid with glasses, plates and cutlery before each of the seventeen chairs. Bottles of bar whisky are placed at intervals within reach of any sitter. An old upright piano and stool have been moved in and stand against the wall at left, front. At right, front, is a table without chairs. The other tables and chairs that had been in the room have been moved out, leaving a clear floor space at rear for dancing. The floor has been swept clean of sawdust and scrubbed. Even the walls show evidence of having been washed, although the result is only to heighten their splotchy leprous look. The electric light brackets are adorned with festoons of red ribbon. In the middle of the separate table at right, front, is a birthday cake with six candles. Several packages, tied with ribbon, are also on the table. There are two necktie boxes, two cigar boxes, a fifth containing a half-dozen handkerchiefs, the sixth is a square jeweller's watch box.

As the curtain rises, CORA, CHUCK, HUGO, LARRY, MARGIE, PEARL *and* ROCKY *are discovered.* CHUCK, ROCKY *and the three girls have dressed up for the occasion.* CORA *is arranging a bouquet of flowers in a vase, the vase being a big schooner glass from the bar, on top of the piano.* CHUCK *sits in a chair at the foot (left) of the banquet table. He has turned it so he can watch her. Near the middle of the row of chairs behind the table,* LARRY *sits, facing front, a drink of whisky before him. He is staring before him in frowning, disturbed meditation. Next to him, on his left,* HUGO *is in his habitual position, passed out, arms on table, head on arms, a full whisky glass by his head. By the separate table at right, front,* MARGIE *and* PEARL *are arranging the cake and presents, and* ROCKY *stands by them. All of them, with the exception of* CHUCK *and* ROCKY, *have had plenty to drink and show it, but no one, except* HUGO, *seems to be drunk. They are trying to act up in the spirit of the occasion but there is something forced about their manner, an undercurrent of nervous irritation and preoccupation.*

CORA (*standing back from the piano to regard the flower effect*). How's dat, Kid?

CHUCK (*grumpily*). What de hell do I know about flowers?

CORA. Yuh can see dey're pretty, can't yuh, yuh big dummy?

CHUCK (*mollifyingly*). Yeah, Baby, sure. If yuh like 'em, dey're aw right wid me.

CORA *goes back to give the schooner of flowers a few more touches.*

MARGIE (*admiring the cake*). Some cake, huh, Poil? Lookit! Six candles. Each for ten years.

PEARL. When do we light de candles, Rocky?

ROCKY (*grumpily*). Ask dat bughouse Hickey. He's elected himself boss of dis boithday racket. Just before Harry comes down, he says. Den Harry blows dem out wid one breath, for luck. Hickey was goin' to have sixty candles, but I says, Jees, if de old guy took dat big a breath, he'd croak himself.

MARGIE (*challengingly*). Well, anyways, it's some cake, ain't it?

ROCKY (*without enthusiasm*). Sure, it's aw right by me. But what de hell is Harry goin' to do wid a cake? If he ever et a hunk, it'd croak him.

PEARL. Jees, yuh're a dope! Ain't he, Margie?

MARGIE. A dope is right!

ROCKY (*stung*). You broads better watch your step or –

PEARL (*defiantly*). Or what?

MARGIE. Yeah! Or what?

They glare at him truculently.

ROCKY. Say, what de hell's got into youse? It'll be twelve o'clock and Harry's boithday before long. I ain't lookin' for no trouble.

PEARL (*ashamed*). Aw, we ain't neider, Rocky.

For the moment this argument subsides.

CORA (*over her shoulder to CHUCK – acidly*). A guy what can't see flowers is pretty must be some dumb-bell.

CHUCK. Yeah? Well, if I was as dumb as you – (*Then mollifyingly.*) Jees, yuh got your scrappin' pants on, ain't yuh? (*Grins good-naturedly.*) Hell, Baby, what's eatin' yuh? All I'm tinkin' is, flowers is dat louse Hickey's stunt. We never had no flowers for Harry's boithday before. What de hell can Harry do wid flowers? He don't know a cauliflower from a geranium.

ROCKY. Yeah, Chuck, it's like I'm tellin' dese broads about de cake. Dat's Hickey's wrinkle, too. (*Bitterly.*) Jees, ever since he woke up, yuh can't hold him. He's taken on de party like it was his boithday.

MARGIE. Well, he's payin' for everything, ain't he?

ROCKY. Aw, I don't mind de boithday stuff so much. What gets my goat is de way he's tryin' to run de whole dump and everyone in it. He's buttin' in all over de place, tellin' everybody where dey get off. On'y he don't really tell yuh. He just keeps hintin' around.

PEARL. Yeah. He was hintin' to me and Margie.

MARGIE. Yeah, de lousy drummer.

ROCKY. He just gives yuh an earful of dat line of bull about yuh got to be honest wid yourself and not kid yourself, and have de guts to be what yuh are. I got sore. I told him dat's aw right for de bums in dis dump. I hope he makes dem wake up. I'm sick of listenin' to dem hop demselves up. But it don't go wid me, see? I don't kid myself wid no pipe dream. (PEARL *and* MARGIE *exchange a derisive look. He catches it and his eyes narrow.*) What are yuh grinnin' at?

PEARL (*her face hard – scornfully*). Nuttin'.

MARGIE. Nuttin'.

ROCKY. It better be nuttin'! Don't let Hickey put no ideas in your nuts if you wanta stay healthy! (*Then angrily.*) I wish de louse never showed up! I hope he don't come back from de delicatessen. He's getting' everyone nuts. He's ridin' someone every minute. He's got Harry and Jimmy Tomorrow run ragged, and de rest is hidin' in deir rooms so dey won't have to listen to him. Dey're all actin' cagey wid de booze, too, like dey was scared if dey get too drunk, dey might spill deir guts, or somethin'. And anybody's bettin' a prize grouch on.

CORA. Yeah, he's been hintin' round to me and Chuck, too. Yuh'd tink he suspected me and Chuck hadn't no real intention of gettin' married. Yuh'd tink he suspected Chuck wasn't goin' to lay off periodicals – or maybe even didn't want to.

CHUCK. He didn't say it right out or I'da socked him one. I told him, 'I'm on de wagon for keeps and Cora knows it.'

CORA. I told him, 'Sure, I know it. And Chuck ain't never goin' to trow it in my face dat I was a tart, neider. And if yuh tink we're just kiddin' ourselves, we'll show yuh!'

CHUCK. We're goin' to show him!

CORA. We got it all fixed. We've decided Joisey is where we want de farm, and we'll get married dere, too, because yuh don't need no licence. We're goin' to get married tomorrow. Ain't we, Honey?

CHUCK. You bet, Baby.

ROCKY (*disgusted*). Christ, Chuck, are yuh lettin' dat bughouse louse Hickey kid yuh into –

CORA (*turns on him angrily*). Nobody's kiddin' him into it, nor me neider! and Hickey's right. If dis big tramp's goin' to marry me, he ought to do it, and not just shoot off his old bazoo about it.

ROCKY (*ignoring her*). Yuh can't be dat dumb, Chuck.

CORA. You keep outa dis! And don't start beefin' about crickets on de farm drivin' us nuts. You and your crickets! Yuh'd tink dey was elephants!

MARGIE (*coming to ROCKY's defence – sneeringly*). Don't notice dat broad, Rocky. Yuh heard her say 'tomorrow,' didn't yuh? It's de same old crap.

CORA (*glares at her*). Is dat so?

PEARL (*lines up with MARGIE – sneeringly*). Imagine Cora a bride! Dat's a hot one! Jees, Cora, if all de guys you've stayed wid was side by side, yuh could walk on 'em from here to Texas!

CORA (*starts moving toward her threateningly*). Yuh can't talk like dat to me, yuh fat Dago hooker! I may be a tart, but I ain't a cheap old whore like you!

PEARL (*furiously*). I'll show yuh who's a whore!

They start to fly at each other, but CHUCK and ROCKY grab them from behind.

CHUCK (*forcing CORA on to a chair*). Sit down and cool off, Baby.

ROCKY (*doing the same to PEARL*). Nix on de rough stuff, Poil.

MARGIE (*glaring at CORA*). Why don't you leave Poil alone, Rocky? She'll fix dat blonde's clock! Or if she don't, I will!

ROCKY. Shut up, you! (*Disgustedly.*) Jees, what dames! D'yuh wanta gum Harry's party?

PEARL (*a bit shamefaced – sulkily*). Who wants to? But nobody can't call me a –

ROCKY (*exasperatedly*). Aw, bury it! What are you, a voigin?

PEARL *stares at him, her face growing hard and bitter. So does.*
MARGIE.

PEARL. Yuh mean you tink I'm a whore, too, huh?

MARGIE. Yeah, and me?

ROCKY. Now don't start nuttin'!

PEARL. I suppose it'd tickle you if me and Margie did what dat louse, Hickey, was hintin' and come right out and admitted we was whores.

ROCKY. Aw right! What of it? It's de truth, ain't it?

CORA (*lining up with PEARL and MARGIE – indignantly*). Jees, Rocky, dat's a fine hell of a ting to say to two goils dat's been as good to yuh as Poil and Margie! (*To PEARL.*) I didn't mean to call yuh dat, Poil. I was on'y mad.

PEARL (*accepts the apology gratefully*). Sure, I was mad, too, Cora. No hard feelin's.

ROCKY (*relieved*). Dere. Dat fixes everything, don't it?

PEARL (*turns on him – hard and bitter*). Aw right, Rocky. We're whores. You know what dat makes you, don't you?

ROCKY (*angrily*). Look out, now!

MARGIE. A lousy little pimp, dat's what!

ROCKY. I'll loin yuh! (*He gives her a slap on the side of the face.*)

PEARL. A dirty little Ginny pimp, dat's what!

ROCKY (*gives her a slap, too*). And dat'll loin you!

But they only stare at him with hard sneering eyes.

MARGIE. He's provin' it to us, Poil.

PEARL. Yeah! Hickey's convoited him. He's give up his pipe dream!

ROCKY (*furious and at the same time bewildered by their defiance*). Lay off me or I'll beat de hell –

CHUCK (*growls*). Aw, lay off dem. Harry's party ain't no time to beat up your stable.

ROCKY (*turns to him*). Whose stable? Who d'yuh tink yuh're

talkin' to? I ain't never beat dem up! What d'yuh tink I am? I just give dem a slap, like any guy would his wife, if she got too gabby. Why don't yuh tell dem to lay off me? I don't want no trouble on Harry's boithday party.

MARGIE (*a victorious gleam in her eye – tauntingly*). Aw right, den, yuh poor little Ginny. I'll lay off yuh till de party's over if Poil will.

PEARL (*tauntingly*). Sure, I will. For Harry's sake, not yours, yuh little Wop!

ROCKY (*stung*). Say, listen, youse! Don't get no wrong idea –

But an interruption comes from LARRY, *who bursts into a sardonic laugh. They all jump startledly and look at him with unanimous hostility.* ROCKY *transfers his anger to him.*

Who de hell yuh laughin' at, yuh half-dead old stew bum?

CORA (*sneeringly*). At himself, he ought to be! Jees, Hickey's sure got his number!

LARRY (*ignoring them, turns to* HUGO *and shakes him by the shoulders – in his comically intense, crazy whisper*). Wake up, Comrade! Here's the Revolution starting on all sides of you and you're sleeping through it! Be God, it's not to Bakunin's ghost you ought to pray in your dreams, but to the great Nihilist, Hickey! He's started a movement that'll blow up the world!

HUGO (*blinks at him through his thick spectacles – with guttural denunciation*). You, Larry! Renegade! Traitor! I vill have you shot! (*He giggles.*) Don't be a fool! Buy me a trink! (*He sees the drink in front of him, and gulps it down. He begins to sing the Carmagnole in a guttural basso, pounding on the table with his glass.*) 'Dansons la Carmagnole! Vive le son! Vive le son! Dansons la Carmagnole! Vive le son des canons!'

ROCKY. Can dat noise!

HUGO (*ignores this – to* LARRY, *in a low tone of hatred*). That bourgeois svine, Hickey! He laughs like good fellow, he makes jokes, he dares make hints to me so I see what he dares to think. He thinks I am finish, it is too late, and so I do not vish the Day come because it vill not be my Day. Oh, I see what he thinks! He thinks lies even vorse, dat I – (*He stops abruptly with a guilty look, as if afraid he was letting something slip – then revengefully.*) I vill have him hanged the first one of all on de first lamp-post! (*He changes his mood abruptly and peers around at* ROCKY *and the others – giggling again.*) Vhy you so serious, leedle monkey-faces? It's all great joke, no? So ve get drunk, and ve laugh like hell, and den ve die, and de pipe dream vanish! (*A bitter mocking contempt creeps into his tone.*) But be of good cheer, leedle stupid peoples! 'The days grow hot, O Babylon!' Soon, leedle proletarians, ve vill have free picnic in the cool shade, ve vill eat hot dogs and trink free beer beneath the villow trees! Like hogs, yes! Like beautiful leedle hogs! (*He stops startledly, as if confused and amazed at what he has heard himself say. He mutters with hatred.*) Dot Gottamned liar, Hickey. It is he who makes me sneer. I want to sleep. (*He lets his head fall forward on his folded arms again and closes his eyes.*)

LARRY *gives him a pitying look, then quickly drinks his drink.*

CORA (*uneasily*). Hickey ain't overlookin' no bets, is he? He's even give Hugo de woiks.

LARRY. I warned you this morning he wasn't kidding.

MARGIE (*sneering*). De old wise guy!

PEARL. Yeah, still pretendin' he's de one exception, like Hickey told him. He don't do no pipe dreamin'! Oh, no!

LARRY (*sharply resentful*). I – ! (*Then abruptly he is drunkenly good-natured, and you feel this drunken manner is an evasive exaggeration.*) All right, take it out on me, if it makes you more content. Sure, I love every hair of your heads, my great big beautiful baby dolls, and there's nothing I wouldn't do for you!

PEARL (*stiffly*). De old Irish bunk, huh? We ain't big. And we ain't your baby dolls! (*Suddenly she is mollified and smiles.*) But we admit we're beautiful. Huh, Margie?

MARGIE (*smiling*). Sure ting! But what would he do wid beautiful dolls, even if he had de price, de old goat? (*She laughs teasingly – then pats* LARRY *on the shoulder affectionately.*) Aw, yuh're aw right at dat, Larry, if yuh are full of bull!

PEARL. Sure. Yuh're aces wid us. We're noivous, dat's all. Dat lousy drummer – why can't he be like he's always been? I never seen a guy change so. You pretend to be such a fox, Larry. What d'yuh tink's happened to him?

LARRY. I don't know. With all his gab I notice he's kept that to himself so far. Maybe he's saving the great revelation for Harry's party. (*Then irritably.*) To hell with him! I don't want to know. Let him mind his own business and I'll mind mine.

CHUCK. Yeah, dat's what I say.

CORA. Say, Larry, where's dat young friend of yours disappeared to?

LARRY. I don't care where he is, except I wish it was a thousand miles away! (*Then, as he sees they are surprised at his vehemence, he adds hastily.*) He's a pest.

ROCKY (*breaks in with his own preoccupation*). I don't give a damn what happened to Hickey, but I know what's gonna happen if he don't watch his step. I told him, 'I'll take a lot from you, Hickey, like everyone else in dis dump, because yuh've always been a grand guy. But dere's tings I don't take from you nor nobody, see? Remember dat, or you'll wake up in a hospital – or maybe worse, wid your wife and de iceman walkin' slow behind yuh.'

CORA. Aw, yuh shouldn't make dat iceman crack, Rocky. It's aw right for him to kid about it but – I notice Hickey ain't pulled dat old iceman gag dis time. (*Excitedly.*) D'yuh suppose dat he did catch his wife cheatin'? I don't mean wid no iceman, but wid som guy.

ROCKY. Aw, dat's de bunk. He ain't pulled dat gag or showed her photo around because he ain't drunk. And if he'd caught her cheatin' he'd be drunk, wouldn't he? He'd have beat her up and den gone on de woist drunk he'd ever staged. Like any other guy'd do.

The girls nod, convinced by this reasoning.

CHUCK. Sure! Rocky's got de right dope, Baby. He'd be paralysed.

While he is speaking, the Negro, JOE, comes in from the hallway. There is a noticeable change in him. He walks with a tough, truculent swagger and his good-natured face is set in sullen suspicion.

JOE (*to ROCKY – defiantly*). I's stood tellin' people dis dump is closed for de night all I's goin' to. Let Harry hire a doorman, pay him wages, if he wants one.

ROCKY (*scowling*). Yeah? Harry's pretty damned good to you.

JOE (*shamefaced*). Sure he is. I don't mean dat. Anyways, it's all right. I told Schwartz, de cop, we's closed for de party. He'll keep folks away. (*Aggressively again.*) I want a big drink, dat's what!

CHUCK. Who's stoppin' yuh? Yuh can have all yuh want on Hickey.

JOE (*has taken a glass from the table and has his hand on a bottle when* HICKEY's *name is mentioned. He draws his hand back as if he were going to refuse – then grabs it defiantly and pours a big drink*). All right, I'd earned all de drinks on him I could drink in a year for listenin' to his crazy bull. And here's hopin' he gets de lockjaw! (*He drinks and pours out another.*) I drinks on him but I don't drink wid him. No, suh, never no more!

ROCKY. Aw, bull! Hickey's aw right. What's he done to you?

JOE (*sullenly*). Dat's my business. I ain't buttin' in yours, is I? (*Bitterly.*) Sure, you think he's all right. He's a white man, ain't he? (*His tone becomes aggressive.*) Listen to me, you white boys! Don't you get it in your heads I's pretendin' to be what I ain't, or dat I ain't proud to be what I is, get me? Or you and me's goin' to have trouble! (*He picks up his drink and walks left as far away from them as he can get and slumps down on the piano stool.*)

MARGIE (*in a low angry tone*). What a noive! Just because we act nice to him, he gets a swelled nut! If dat ain't a coon all over!

CHUCK. Talkin' fight talk, huh? I'll moider de nigger! (*He takes a threatening step toward* JOE, *who is staring before him guiltily now.*)

JOE (*speaks up shamefacedly*). Listen, boys, I's sorry. I didn't mean dat. You been good friends to me. I's nuts, I guess. Dat Hickey, he gets my head all mixed up wit craziness.

Their faces at once clear of resentment against him.

CORA. Aw, dat's aw right, Joe. De boys wasn't takin' yuh serious. (*Then to the others, forcing a laugh.*) Jees, what'd I say, Hickey ain't overlookin' no bets. Even Joe. (*She pauses – then adds puzzledly.*) De funny ting is yuh can't stay sore at de bum when he's around. When he forgets de bughouse preachin', and quits tellin' yuh where yuh get off, he's de same old Hickey. Yuh can't help likin' de louse. And yuh got to admit he's got de right dope – (*She adds hastily.*) I mean, on some of de bums here.

MARGIE (*with a sneering look at* ROCKY). Yeah, he's coitinly got one guy I know sized up right! Huh, Poil?

PEARL. He coitinly has!

ROCKY. Cut it out, I told yuh!

LARRY (*is staring before him broodingly. He speaks more aloud to himself than to them*). It's nothing to me what happened to him. But I have a feeling he's dying to tell us, inside him, and yet he's afraid. He's like that damned kid. It's strange the queer way he seems to recognize him. If he's afraid, it explains why he's off booze. Like that damned kid again. Afraid if he got drunk, he'd tell –

While he is speaking, HICKEY *comes in the doorway at rear. He looks the same as in the previous act, except that now his face beams with the excited expectation of a boy going to a party. His arms are piled with packages.*

HICKEY (*booms in imitation of a familiar Polo Grounds bleacherite cry – with rising volume*). Well! Well!! Well!!! (*They all jump startledly. He comes forward, grinning.*) Here I am in the nick of time. Give me a hand with these bundles, somebody.

MARGIE *and* PEARL *start taking them from his arms and putting them on the table. Now that he is present, all their attitudes show the reaction* CORA *has expressed. They can't help liking him and forgiving him.*

MARGIE. Jees, Hickey, yuh scared me outa a year's growth, sneakin' in like dat.

HICKEY. Sneaking? Why, me and the taxi man made enough noise getting my big surprise in the hall to wake the dead. You were all so busy drinking in words of wisdom from the Old Wise Guy here, you couldn't hear anything else. (*He grins at* LARRY.) From what I heard, Larry, you're not so good when you start playing Sherlock Holmes. You've got me all wrong. I'm not afraid of anything now – not even myself. You better stick to the part of Old Cemetery, the Barker for the Big Sleep – that is, if you can still let yourself get away with it! (*He chuckles and gives* LARRY *a friendly slap on the back.*)

LARRY *gives him a bitter angry look.*

CORA (*giggles*). Old Cemetery! That's him, Hickey. We'll have to call him dat.

HICKEY (*watching* LARRY *quizzically*). Beginning to do a lot of puzzling about me, aren"t you Larry? But that won't help you. You've got to think of yourself. I couldn't give you my peace. You've got to find your own. All I can do is help you, and the rest of the gang, by showing you the way to find it. (*He has said this with a simple persuasive earnestness. He pauses, and for a second they stare at him with fascinated resentful uneasiness.*)

ROCKY (*breaks the spell*). Aw, hire a church!

HICKEY (*placatingly*). All right! All right! Don't get sore, boys and girls. I guess that did sound too much like a lousy preacher. Let's forget it and get busy on the party.

They look relieved.

CHUCK. Is dose bundles grub, Hickey? You bought enough already to feed an army.

HICKEY (*with boyish excitement again*). Can't be too much! I want this to be the biggest birthday Harry's ever had. You and Rocky go in the hall and get the big surprise. My arms are busted lugging it.

They catch his excitement. CHUCK *and* ROCKY *go out, grinning expectantly. The three girls gather around* HICKEY, *full of thrilled curiosity.*

PEARL. Jees, yuh got us all het up! What is it, Hickey?

HICKEY. Wait and see. I got it as a treat for the three of you more than anyone. I thought to myself, I'll bet this is what will please those whores more than anything. (*They wince as if he had slapped them, but before they have a chance to be angry, he goes on affectionately.*) I said to myself, I don't care how much it costs, they're worth it. They're the best little scouts in the world, and they've been damned kind to me when I was down and out! Nothing is too good for them. (*Earnestly.*) I mean every word of that, too – and then some! (*Then, as if he noticed the expression on their faces for the first time.*) What's the matter? You look sore. What – (*Then he chuckles.*) Oh, I see. But you know how I feel about that. You know I didn't say it to offend you. So don't be silly now.

MARGIE (*lets out a tense breath*). Aw right, Hickey. Let it slide.

HICKEY (*jubilantly, as* CHUCK *and* ROCKY *enter carrying a big wicker basket*). Look! There it comes! Unveil it, boys.

They pull off a covering burlap bag. The basket is piled with quarts of champagne.

PEARL (*with childish excitement*). It's champagne! Jees, Hickey, if you ain't a sport! (*She gives him a hug, forgetting all animosity, as do the other girls.*)

MARGIE. I never been soused on champagne. Let's get stinko, Poil.

PEARL. You betcha my life! De bot' of us!

A holiday spirit of gay festivity has seized them all. Even JOE MOTT *is standing up to look at the wine with an admiring grin, and* HUGO *raises his head to blink at it.*

JOE. You sure is hittin' de high spots, Hickey. (*Boastfully.*) Man, when I runs my gamblin' house, I drinks dat old bubbly water in steins! (*He stops guiltily and gives* HICKEY *a look of defiance.*) I's goin' to drink it dat way again, too, soon's I make my stake! And dat ain't no pipe dream, neider! (*He sits down where he was, his back turned to them.*)

ROCKY. What'll we drink it outa, Hickey? Dere ain't no wine glasses.

HICKEY (*enthusiastically*). Joe has the right idea! Schooners! That's the spirit for Harry's birthday!

ROCKY *and* CHUCK *carry the basket of wine into the bar. The three girls go back and stand around the entrance to the bar, chatting excitedly among themselves and to* CHUCK *and* ROCKY *in the bar.*

HUGO (*with his silly giggle*). Ve vill trink vine beneath the villow trees!

HICKEY (*grins at him*). That's the spirit, Brother – and let the lousy slaves drink vinegar!

HUGO *blinks at him startledly, then looks away.*

HUGO (*mutters*). Gottamned liar! (*He puts his head back on his arms and closes his eyes, but this time his habitual pass-out has a quality of hiding.*)

LARRY (*gives* HUGO *a pitying glance – in a low tone of anger*). Leave Hugo be! He rotted ten years in prison for his faith! He's earned his dream! Have you no decency or pity?

HICKEY (*quizzically*). Hello, what's this? I thought you were in the grandstand. (*Then with a simple earnestness, taking a chair by* LARRY, *and putting a hand on his shoulder.*) Listen, Larry, you're getting me all wrong. Hell, you ought to know me better. I've always been the best-natured slob in the world. Of course, I have pity. But now I've seen the light, it isn't my old kind of pity – the kind yours is. It isn't the kind that lets itself off easy by encouraging some poor guy to go on kidding himself with a lie – the kind that leaves the poor slob worse off because it makes him feel guiltier than ever – the kind that makes his lying hopes nag at him and reproach him until he's a rotten skunk in his own eyes. I know all about that kind of pity. I've had a bellyful of it in my time, and it's all wrong! (*With a salesman's persuasiveness.*) No, sir. The kind of pity I feel now is after final results that will really save the poor guy, and make him contented with what he is, and quit battling himself, and find peace for the rest of his life. Oh, I know how you resent the way I have to show you up to yourself. I don't blame you. I know from my own experience it's bitter medicine, facing yourself in the mirror with the old false whiskers off. But you forget that, once you're cured. You'll be grateful to me when all at once you find you're able to admit, without feeling ashamed, that all the grandstand foolosopher bunk and the waiting for the Big Sleep stuff is a pipe dream. You'll say to yourself, I'm just an old man who is scared of life, but even more scared of dying. So I'm keeping drunk and hanging on to life at any price, and what of it? Then you'll know what real peace means, Larry, because you won't be scared of either life or death any more. You simply won't give a damn! Any more than I do!

LARRY (*has been staring into his eyes with a fascinated wondering dread*). Be God, if I'm not beginning to think you've gone mad! (*With a rush of anger.*) You're a liar!

HICKEY (*injuredly*). Now, listen, that's no way to talk to an old pal who's trying to help you. Hell, if you really wanted to die, you'd just take a hop off your fire escape, wouldn't you? And if you really were in the grandstand, you wouldn't be pitying everyone. Oh, I know the truth is tough at first. It was for me. All I ask is for you to suspend judgment and give it a chance. I'll absolutely guarantee – Hell, Larry, I'm no fool. Do you suppose I'd deliberately set out to get under everyone's skin and put myself in dutch with all my old pals, if I wasn't certain, from my own experience, that it means contentment in the end for all of you? (LARRY *again is staring at him fascinateedly.* HICKEY *grins.*) As for my being bughouse, you can't crawl out of it that way. Hell, I'm too damned sane. I can size up guys, and turn 'em inside out, better than I ever could. Even where they're strangers like that Parritt kid. He's licked, Larry. I think there is only one possible way out you can help him to take. That is, if you have the right kind of pity for him.

LARRY (*uneasily*). What do you mean? (*Attempting indifference.*) I'm not advising him, except to leave me out of his troubles. He's nothing to me.

HICKEY (*shakes his head*). You'll find he won't agree to that. He'll keep after you until he makes you help him. Because he has to be punished, so he can forgive himself. He's lost all his guts. He can't manage it alone, and you're the only one he can turn to.

LARRY. For the love of God, mind your own business! (*With forced scorn.*) A lot you know about him! He's hardly spoken to you!

HICKEY. No, that's right. But I do know a lot about him just the same. I've had hell inside me. I can spot it in others. (*Frowning.*) Maybe that's what gives me the feeling there's something familiar about him, something between us. (*He shakes his head.*) No, it's more than that. I can't figure it. Tell me about him. For instance, I don't imagine he's married, is he?

LARRY. No.

HICKEY. Hasn't he been mixed up with some woman? I don't mean trollops. I mean the old real love stuff that crucifies you.

LARRY (*with a calculating relieved look at him – encouraging him along this line*). Maybe you're right. I wouldn't be surprised.

HICKEY (*grins at him quizzically*). I see. You think I'm on the wrong track and you're glad I am. Because then I won't suspect whatever he did about the Great Cause. That's another lie you tell yourself, Larry, that the good old Cause means nothing to you any more. (LARRY *is about to burst out in denial but* HICKEY *goes on,*) But you're all wrong about Parritt. That isn't what's behind that. And it's a woman. I recognize the symptoms.

LARRY (*sneeringly*). And you're the boy who's never wrong! Don't be a damned fool. His trouble is he was brought up a devout believer in the Movement and now he's lost his faith. It's a shock, but he's young and he'll soon find another dream just as good. (*He adds sardonically.*) Or as bad.

HICKEY. All right. I'll let it go at that, Larry. He's nothing to me except I'm glad he's here because he'll help me make you wake up to yourself. I don't even like the guy, or the feeling there's anything between us. But you'll find I'm right just the same, when you get to the final showdown with him.

LARRY. There'll be no showdown! I don't give a tinker's damn –

HICKEY. Sticking to the old grandstand, eh? Well, I knew you'd be the toughest to convince of all the gang, Larry. And, along with Harry and Jimmy Tomorrow, you're the one I want most to help. (*He puts an arm around* LARRY's *shoulder and gives him an affectionate hug.*) I've always liked you a lot, you old bastard! (*He gets up and his manner changes to his bustling party excitement – glancing at his watch.*) Well, well, not much time before twelve. Let's get busy, boys and girls. (*He looks over the table where the cake is.*) Cake all set. Good. And my presents, and yours, girls, and Chuck's, and Rocky's. Fine. Harry'll certainly be touched by your thought of him. (*He goes back to the girls.*) You go in the

bar, Pearl and Margie, and get the grub ready so it can be
brought right in. There'll be some drinking and toasts first, of
course. My idea is to use the wine for that, so get it all set. I'll
go upstairs now and root everyone out. Harry the last. I'll come
back with him. Somebody light the candles on the cake when
you hear us coming, and you start playing Harry's favourite
tune, Cora. Hustle now, everybody. We want this to come off in
style.

*He bustles into the hall. MARGIE and PEARL disappear in the bar.
CORA goes to the piano. JOE gets off the stool sullenly to let her sit
down.*

CORA. I got to practise. I ain't laid my mits on a box in Gawd
knows when. (*With the soft pedal down, she begins gropingly to pick
out 'The Sunshine of Paradise Alley'.*) Is dat right, Joe? I've
forgotten dat has-been tune. (*She picks out a few more notes.*)
Come on, Joe, hum de tune so I can follow.

*JOE begins to hum and sing in a low voice and correct her. He forgets
his sullenness and becomes his old self again.*

LARRY (*suddenly gives a laugh – in his comically intense, crazy tone*).
Be God, it's a second feast of Belshazzar, with Hickey to do the
writing on the wall!

CORA. Aw, shut up, Old Cemetery! Always beefin'!

*WILLIE comes in from the hall. He is in a pitiable state, his face
pasty, haggard with sleeplessness and nerves, his eyes sick and haunted.
He is sober. CORA greets him over her shoulder kiddingly.*

If it ain't Prince Willie! (*Then kindly.*) Gee, kid, yuh look sick.
Git a coupla shots in yuh.

WILLIE (*tensely*). No, thanks, Not now. I'm tapering off. (*He sits
down weakly on LARRY's right.*)

CORA (*astonished*). What d'yuh know? He means it!

WILLIE (*leaning toward LARRY confidentially – in a low shaken
voice*). It's been hell up in that damned room, Larry! The things
I've imagined! (*He shudders.*) I thought I'd go crazy. (*With
pathetic boastful pride.*) But I've got it beat now. By tomorrow
morning I'll be on the wagon. I'll get back my clothes the first
thing. Hickey's loaning me the money. I'm going to do what
I've always said – go to the DA's office. He was a good friend
of my Old Man's. He was only assistant, then. He was in on the
graft, but my Old Man never squealed on him. So he certainly
owes it to me to give me a chance. And he knows that I really

was a brilliant law student. (*Self-reassuringly.*) Oh, I know I can make good, now I'm getting off the booze for ever. (*Moved.*) I owe a lot to Hickey. He's made me wake up to myself – see what a fool – It wasn't nice to face but – (*With bitter resentment.*) It isn't what he says. It's what you feel behind – what he hints – Christ, you'd think all I really wanted to do with my life was sit here and stay drunk. (*With hatred.*) I'll show him!

LARRY (*masking pity behind a sardonic tone*). If you want my advice, you'll put the nearest bottle to your mouth until you don't give a damn for Hickey!

WILLIE (*stares at a bottle greedily, tempted for a moment – then bitterly*). That's fine advice! I thought you were my friend! (*He gets up with a hurt glance at LARRY, and moves away to take a chair in back of the left end of the table, where he sits in dejected, shaking misery, his chin on his chest.*)

JOE (*to CORA*). No, like dis. (*He beats time with his finger and sings in a low voice.*) 'She is the sunshine of Paradise Alley.' (*She plays.*) Dat's more like it. Try it again.

She begins to play through the chorus again. DON PARRITT enters from the hall. There is a frightened look on his face. He slinks in furtively, as if he were escaping from someone. He looks relieved when he sees LARRY and comes and slips into the chair on his right. LARRY pretends not to notice his coming, but he instinctively shrinks with repulsion. PARRITT leans toward him and speaks ingratiatingly in a low secretive tone.

PARRITT. Gee, I'm glad you're here, Larry. That damned fool, Hickey, knocked on my door. I opened up because I thought it must be you, and he came busting in and made me come downstairs. I don't know what for. I don't belong in this birthday celebration. I don't know this gang and I don't want to be mixed up with them. All I came here for was to find you.

LARRY (*tensely*). I've warned you –

PARRITT (*goes on as if he hadn't heard*). Can't you make Hickey mind his own business? I don't like that guy, Larry. The way he acts, you'd think he had something on me. Why, just now he pats me on the shoulder, like he was sympathizing with me, and says, 'I know how it is, Son, but you can't hide from yourself, not even here on the bottom of the sea. You've got to face the truth and then do what must be done for your own peace and the happiness of all concerned.' What did he mean by that, Larry?

LARRY. How the hell would I know?

PARRITT. Then he grins and says, 'Never mind, Larry's getting wise to himself. I think you can rely on his help in the end. He'll have to choose between living and dying, and he'll never choose to die while there is a breath left in the old bastard!' And then he laughs like it was a joke on you. (*He pauses. LARRY is rigid on his chair, staring before him. PARRITT asks him with a sudden taunt in his voice.*) Well, what do you say to that, Larry?

LARRY. I've nothing to say. Except you're a bigger fool than he is to listen to him.

PARRITT (*with a sneer*). Is that so? He's no fool where you're concerned. He's got your number, all right! (*LARRY's face tightens but he keeps silent. PARRITT changes to a contrite, appealing air.*) I don't mean that. But you keep acting as if you were sore at me, and that gets my goat. You know what I want most is to be friends with you, Larry. I haven't a single friend left in the world, I hoped you – (*Bitterly.*) And you could be, too, without it hurting you. You ought to, for Mother's sake. She really loved you. You loved her, too, didn't you?

LARRY (*tensely*). Leave what's dead in its grave.

PARRITT. I suppose, because I was only a kid, you didn't think I was wise about you and her. Well, I was. I've been wise, ever since I can remember, to all the guys she's had, although she'd tried to kid me along it wasn't so. That was a silly stunt for a free Anarchist woman, wasn't it, being ashamed of being free?

LARRY. Shut your damned trap!

PARRITT (*guiltily but with a strange undertone of satisfaction*). Yes, I know I shouldn't say that now. I keep forgetting she isn't free any more. (*He pauses.*) Do you know, Larry, you're the one of them all she cared most about? Anyone else who left the Movement would have been dead to her, but she couldn't forget you. She'd always made excuses for you. I used to try and get her goat about you. I'd say, 'Larry's got brains and yet he thinks the Movement is just a crazy pipe dream.' She'd blame it on booze getting you. She'd kid herself that you'd give up booze and come back to the Movement – tomorrow! She'd say, 'Larry can't kill in himself a faith he's given his life to, not without killing himself.' (*He grins sneeringly.*) How about it, Larry? Was she right? (*LARRY remains silent. He goes on insistently.*) I suppose what she really meant was, come back to her. She was always getting the Movement mixed up with herself. But I'm sure she really must have loved you, Larry. As much as she could love anyone besides herself. But she wasn't faithful to you, even at that, was she? That's why you finally walked out on her, isn't it? I remember that last fight you had with her. I was listening. I was on your side, even if she was my mother, because I liked you so much; you'd been so good to me – like a father. I remember her putting on her high-and-mighty free-woman stuff, saying you were still a slave to bourgeois morality and jealousy and you thought a woman you loved was a piece of private property you owned. I remember that you got mad and you told her, 'I don't like living with a whore, if that's what you mean!'

LARRY (*bursts out*). You lie! I never called her that!

PARRITT (*goes on as if LARRY hadn't spoken*). I think that's why she still respects you, because it was you who left her. You were the only one to beat her to it. She got sick of the others before they did of her. I don't think she ever cared much about them, anyway. She just had to keep on having lovers to prove to herself how free she was. (*He pauses – then with a bitter repulsion.*) It made home a lousy place. I felt like you did about it. I'd get feeling it was like living in a whorehouse – only worse, because she didn't have to make her living –

LARRY. You bastard! She's your mother! Have you no shame?

PARRITT (*bitterly*). No! She brought me up to believe that family-respect stuff is all bourgeois, property-owning crap. Why should I be ashamed?

LARRY (*making a move to get up*). I've had enough!

PARRITT (*catches his arm – pleadingly*). No! Don't leave me! Please! I promise I won't mention her again!

LARRY *sinks back in his chair*.

I only did it to make you understand better. I know this isn't the place to – Why didn't you come up to my room, like I asked you? I kept waiting. We could talk everything over there.

LARRY. There's nothing to talk over!

PARRITT. But I've got to talk to you. Or I'll talk to Hickey. He won't let me alone! I feel he knows, anyway! And I know he'd understand, all right – in his way. But I hate his guts! I don't want anything to do with him! I'm scared of him, honest.

There's something not human behind his damned grinning and kidding.

LARRY (*starts*). Ah! You feel that, too?

PARRITT (*pleadingly*). But I can't go on like this. I've got to decide what I've got to do. I've got to tell you, Larry!

LARRY (*again starts up*). I won't listen!

PARRITT (*again holds him by the arm*). All right I won't. Don't go!

LARRY *lets himself be pulled down on his chair.* PARRITT *examines his face and becomes insultingly scornful.*

Who do you think you're kidding? I know damned well you you've guessed –

LARRY. I've guessed nothing!

PARRITT. But I want you to guess now! I'm glad you have! I know now, since Hickey's been after me, that I meant you to guess right from the start. That's why I came to you. (*Hurrying on with an attempt at a plausible frank air that makes what he says seem doubly false.*) I want you to understand the reason. You see, I began studying American history. I got admiring Washington and Jefferson and Jackson and Lincoln. I began to feel patriotic and love this country. I saw it was the best government in the world, where everybody was equal and had a chance. I saw that all the ideas behind the Movement came from a lot of Russians like Bakunin and Kropotkin and were meant for Europe, but we didn't need them here in a democracy where we were free already. I didn't want this country to be destroyed for a damned foreign pipe dream. After all, I'm from old American pioneer stock. I began to feel I was a traitor for helping a lot of cranks and bums and free women plot to overthrow our government. And then I saw it was my duty to my country –

LARRY (*nauseated – turns on him*). You stinking rotten liar! Do you think you can fool me with such hypocrite's cant! (*Then turning away.*) I don't give a damn what you did! It's on your head – whatever it was! I don't want to know – and I won't know!

PARRITT (*as if LARRY had never spoken – falteringly*). But I never thought Mother would be caught. Please believe that, Larry. You know I never would have –

LARRY (*his face haggard, drawing a deep breath and closing his eyes – as if he were trying to hammer something into his own brain*). All I know is I'm sick of life! I'm through! I've forgotten myself! I'm drowned and contented on the bottom of a bottle. Honour or dishonour, faith or treachery are nothing to me but the opposites of the same stupidity which is ruler and king of life, and in the end they rot into dust in the same grave. All things are the same meaningless joke to me, for they grin at me from the one skull of death. So go away. You're wasting breath. I've forgotten your mother.

PARRITT (*jeers angrily*). The old foolosopher, eh? (*He spits out contemptuously.*) You lousy old faker!

LARRY (*so distracted he pleads weakly*). For the love of God, leave me in peace the little time that's left to me!

PARRITT. Aw, don't pull that pitiful old-man junk on me! You old bastard, you'll never die as long as there's a free drink of whisky left!

LARRY (*stung – furiously*). Look out how you try to taunt me back into life, I warn you! I might remember the thing they call justice there, and the punishment for – (*He checks himself with an effort – then with a real indifference that comes from exhaustion.*) I'm old and tired. To hell with you! You're as mad as Hickey, and as big a liar. I'd never let myself believe a word you told me.

PARRITT (*threateningly*). The hell you won't! Wait till Hickey gets through with you!

PEARL *and* MARGIE *come in from the bar. At the sight of them,* PARRITT *instantly subsides and becomes self-conscious and defensive, scowling at them and then quickly looking away.*

MARGIE (*eyes him jeeringly*). Why, hello, Tightwad Kid. Come to join de party? Gee, don't he act bashful, Poil?

PEARL. Yeah. Especially wid his dough.

PARRITT *slinks to a chair at the left end of the table, pretending he hasn't heard them. Suddenly there is a noise of angry, cursing voices and a scuffle from the hall.* PEARL *yells.*

Hey, Rocky! Fight in de hall!

ROCKY *and* CHUCK *run from behind the bar curtain and rush into the hall.* ROCKY's *voice is heard in irritated astonishment,* 'What de hell?' *and then the scuffle stops and* ROCKY *appears holding* CAPTAIN LEWIS *by the arm, followed by* CHUCK *with a similar hold on* GENERAL WETJOEN. *Although these two have been drinking they are both sober, for them. Their faces are sullenly angry, their clothes disarranged from the tussle.*

ROCKY (*leading* LEWIS *forward – astonished, amused and irritated*).
Can yuh beat it? I've heard youse two call each odder every
name yuh could think of but I never seen you – (*Indignantly.*) A
swell time to stage your first bout, on Harry's boithday party!
What started de scrap!

LEWIS (*forcing a casual tone*). Nothing, old chap. Our business,
you know. That bloody ass, Hickey, made some insinuation
about me, and the boorish Boer had the impertinence to agree
with him.

WETJOEN. Dot's a lie! Hickey made joke about me, and this
Limey said yes, it was true!

ROCKY. Well, sit down, de bot' of yuh, and cut out de rough stuff.

He and CHUCK *dump them down in adjoining chairs toward the left
end of the table, where, like two sulky boys, they turn their backs on
each other as far as possible in chairs which both face front.*

MARGIE (*laughs*). Jees, lookit de two bums! Like a coupla kids!
Kiss and make up, for Gawd's sakes!

ROCKY. Yeah. Harry's party begins in a minute and we don't
want no soreheads around.

LEWIS (*stiffly*). Very well, in deference to the occasion, I
apologize, General Wetjoen – provided that you do also.

WETJOEN (*sulkily*). I apologize, Captain Lewis – because Harry is
my goot friend.

ROCKY. Aw, hell! If yuh can't do better'n dat – !

MOSHER *and* MCGLOIN *enter together from the hall. Both have
been drinking but are not drunk.*

PEARL. Here's de star boarders.

*They advance, their heads together, so interested in a discussion they
are oblivious to everyone.*

MCGLOIN. I'm telling you, Ed, it's serious this time. That
bastard, Hickey, has got Harry on the hip.

As he talks, MARGIE, PEARL, ROCKY *and* CHUCK *prick up
their ears and gather round.* CORA, *at the piano keeps running
through the tune, with soft pedal, and singing the chorus half under
her breath, with* JOE *still correcting her mistakes. At the table,*
LARRY, PARRITT, WILLIE, WETJOEN *and* LEWIS *sit
motionless, staring in front of them.* HUGO *seems asleep in his
habitual position.*

And you know it isn't going to do us no good if he gets him to take that walk tomorrow.

MOSHER. You're damned right. Harry'll mosey around the ward, dropping in on everyone who knew him then. (*Indignantly.*) And they'll all give him a phony glad hand and a ton of good advice about what a sucker he is to stand for us.

MCGLOIN. He's sure to call on Bessie's relations to do a little cryin' over dear Bessie. And you know what that bitch and all her family thought of me.

MOSHER (*with a flash of his usual humour – rebukingly*). Remember, Lieutenant, you are speaking of my sister! Dear Bessie wasn't a bitch. She was a God-damned bitch! But if you think my loving relatives will have time to discuss you, you don't know then.. They'll be too busy telling Harry what a drunken crook I am and saying he ought to have me put in Sing Sing!

MCGLOIN (*dejectedly*). Yes, once Bessie's relations get their hooks in him, it'll be as tough for us as if she wasn't gone.

MOSHER (*dejectedly*). Yes, Harry has always been weak and easily influenced, and now he's getting old he'll be an easy mark for those grafters. (*Then with forced reassurance.*) Oh, hell, Mac, we're saps to worry. We've heard Harry pull that bluff about taking a walk every birthday he's had for twenty years.

MCGLOIN (*doubtfully*). But Hickey wasn't sicking him on those times. Just the opposite. He was asking Harry what he wanted to go out for when there was plenty of whisky here.

MOSHER (*with a change to forced carelessness*). Well, after all, I don't care whether he goes out or not. I'm clearing out tomorrow morning anyway. I'm just sorry for you, Mac.

MCGLOIN (*resentfully*). You needn't be, then. Ain't I going myself? I was only feeling sorry for you.

MOSHER. Yes, my mind is made up. Hickey may be a lousy, interfering pest, now he's gone teetotal on us, but there's a lot of truth in some of his bull. Hanging around here getting plastered with you, Mac, is pleasant, I won't deny, but the old booze gets you in the end, if you keep lapping it up. It's time I quit for a while. (*With forced enthusiasm.*) Besides, I feel the call of the old carefree circus life in my blood again. I'll see the boss tomorrow. It's late in the season but he'll be glad to take me on. And won't all the old gang be tickled to death when I show up on the lot!

MCGLOIN. Maybe – if they've got a rope handy!

MOSHER (*turns on him – angrily*). Listen! I'm damned sick of that kidding!

MCGLOIN. You are, are you? Well, I'm sicker of your kidding me about getting reinstated on the Force. And whatever you'd like, I can't spend my life sitting here with you, ruining my stomach with rotgut. I'm tapering off, and in the morning I'll be fresh as a daisy. I'll go and have a private chin with the Commissioner. (*With forced enthusiasm.*) Man alive, from what the boys tell me, there's sugar galore these days, and I'll soon be ridin' around in a big red automobile –

MOSHER (*derisively – beckoning an imaginary Chinese*). Here, One Lung Hop! Put fresh peanut oil in the lamp and cook the Lieutenant another dozen pills! It's his gowed-up night!

MCGLOIN (*stung – pulls back a fist threateningly*). One more crack like that and I'll – !

MOSHER (*putting up his fists*). Yes? Just start –

CHUCK *and* ROCKY *jump between them.*

ROCKY. Hey! Are you guys nuts? Jees, it's Harry's boithday party! (*They both look guilty.*) Sit down and behave.

MOSHER (*grumpily*). All right. Only tell him to lay off me.

He lets ROCKY *push him in a chair, at the right end of the table, rear.*

MCGLOIN (*grumpily*). Tell him to lay off me.

He lets CHUCK *push him into the chair on* MOSHER's *left. At this moment* HICKEY *bursts in from the hall, bustling and excited.*

HICKEY. Everything all set? Fine! (*He glances at his watch.*) Half a minute to go. Harry's starting down with Jimmy. I had a hard time getting them to move! They'd rather stay hiding up there, kidding each other along. (*He chuckles.*) Harry don't even want to remember it's his birthday now! (*He hears a noise from the stairs.*) Here they come! (*Urgently.*) Light the candles! Get ready to play, Cora! Stand up, everybody! Get that wine ready, Chuck and Rocky!

MARGIE *and* PEARL *light the candles on the cake.* CORA *gets her hands set over the piano keys, watching over her shoulder.* ROCKY *and* CHUCK *go in the bar. Everybody at the table stands up mechanically.* HUGO *is the last, suddenly coming to and scrambling to his feet.* HARRY HOPE *and* JIMMY TOMORROW *appear in the hall outside the door.* HICKEY *looks up from his watch.*

On the dot! It's twelve! (*Like a cheer leader.*) Come on now, everybody, with a Happy Birthday, Harry!

With his voice leading they all shout 'Happy, Birthday, Harry!' *in a spiritless chorus.* HICKEY *signals to* CORA, *who starts playing and singing in a whisky soprano* 'She's the Sunshine of Paradise Alley.' HOPE *and* JIMMY *stand in the doorway. Both have been drinking heavily. In* HOPE *the effect is apparent only in a bristling, touchy, pugnacious attitude. It is entirely different from the usual irascible beefing he delights in and which no one takes seriously. Now he really has a chip on his shoulder.* JIMMY, *on the other hand, is plainly drunk, but it has not had the desired effect, for beneath a pathetic assumption of gentlemanly poise, he is obviously frightened and shrinking back within himself.* HICKEY *grabs* HOPE's *hand and pumps it up and down. For a moment* HOPE *appears unconscious of this handshake. Then he jerks his hand away angrily.*

HOPE. Cut out the glad hand, Hickey. D'you think I'm a sucker? I know you, bejees, you sneaking, lying drummer! (*With rising anger, to the others.*) And all you bums! What the hell you trying to do, yelling and raising the roof? Want the cops to close the joint and get my licence taken away? (*He yells at* CORA, *who has stopped singing but continues to play mechanically with many mistakes.*) Hey, you dumb tart, quit banging that box! Bejees, the least you could do is learn the tune!

CORA (*stops – deeply hurt*). Aw, Harry! Jees, ain't I – (*Her eyes begin to fill.*)

HOPE (*glaring at the other girls*). And you two hookers, screaming at the top of your lungs! What d'you think this is, a dollar cathouse? Bejees, that's where you belong!

PEARL (*miserably*). Aw, Harry – (*She begins to cry.*)

MARGIE. Jees, Harry, I never thought you'd say that – like yuh meant it. (*She puts her arm around* PEARL – *on the verge of tears herself.*) Aw, don't bawl, Poil. He don't mean it.

HICKEY (*reproachfully*). Now, Harry! Don't take it out on the gang because you're upset about yourself. Anyway, I've promised you you'll come through all right, haven't I? So quit worrying. (*He slaps* HOPE *on the back encouragingly.* HOPE *flashes him a glance of hate.*) Be yourself, Governor. You don't want to bawl out the old gang just when they're congratulating you on your birthday, do you? Hell, that's no way!

HOPE (*looking guilty and shamefaced now – forcing an unconvincing attempt at his natural tone*). Bejees, they ain't as dumb as you.

They know I was only kidding them. They know I appreciate their congratulations. Don't you, fellers?

There is a listless chorus of 'Sure, Harry,' 'Yes,' 'Of course we do,' *etc. He comes forward to the two girls, with* JIMMY *and* HICKEY *following him, and pats them clumsily.*

Bejees, I like you broads. You know I was only kidding. (*Instantly they forgive him and smile affectionately.*)

MARGIE. Sure we know, Harry.

PEARL. Sure.

HICKEY (*grinning*). Sure. Harry's the greatest kidder in the dump and that's saying something! Look how he's kidded himself for twenty years! (*As* HOPE *gives him a bitter, angry glance, he digs him in the ribs with his elbow playfully.*) Unless I'm wrong, Governor, and I'm betting I'm not. We'll soon know, eh? Tomorrow morning. No, by God, it's *this* morning now!

JIMMY (*with a dazed dread*). *This* morning?

HICKEY. Yes, it's today at last, Jimmy. (*He pats him on the back.*) Don't be so scared! I've promised I'll help you.

JIMMY (*trying to hide his dread behind an offended, drunken dignity*). I don't understand you. Kindly remember I'm fully capable of settling my own affairs!

HICKEY (*earnestly*). Well, isn't that exactly what I want you to do, settle with yourself once and for all? (*He speaks in his ear in confidential warning.*) Only watch out on the booze, Jimmy. You know, not too much from now on. You've had a lot already; and you don't want to let yourself duck out of it by being too drunk to move – not this time!

JIMMY *gives him a guilty, stricken look and turns away and slumps into the chair on* MOSHER's *right.*

HOPE (*to* MARGIE – *still guiltily*). Bejees, Margie, you know I didn't mean it. It's that lousy drummer riding me that's got my goat.

MARGIE. I know. (*She puts a protecting arm around* HOPE *and turns him to face the table with the cake and presents.*) Come on. You ain't noticed your cake yet. Ain't it grand?

HOPE (*trying to brighten up*). Say, that's pretty. Ain't ever had a cake since Bessie – Six candles. Each for ten years, eh? Bejees, that's thoughtful of you.

PEARL. It was Hickey got it.

HOPE (*his tone forced*). Well, it was thoughtful of him. He means well, I guess. (*His eyes, fixed on the cake, harden angrily.*) To hell with his cake. (*He starts to turn away.*)

PEARL *grabs his arm.*

PEARL. Wait, Harry. Yuh ain't seen de presents from Margie and me and Cora and Chuck and Rocky. And dere's a watch all engraved wid your name and de date from Hickey.

HOPE. To hell with it! Bejees, he can keep it! (*This time he does turn away.*)

PEARL. Jees, he ain't even goin' to look at our presents.

MARGIE (*bitterly*). Dis is all wrong. We gotta put some life in dis party or I'll go nuts! Hey, Cora, what's de matter wid dat box? Can't yuh play for Harry? Yuh don't have to stop just because he kidded yuh!

HOPE (*rouses himself – with forced heartiness*). Yes, come on, Cora. You was playing it fine.

CORA *begins to play half-heartedly.* HOPE *suddenly becomes almost tearfully sentimental.*

It was Bessie's favourite tune. She was always singing it. It brings her back. I wish – (*He chokes up.*)

HICKEY (*grins at him – amusedly*). Yes, we've all heard you tell us you thought the world of her, Governor.

HOPE (*looks at him with frightened suspicion*). Well, so I did, bejees! Everyone knows I did! (*Threateningly.*) Bejees, if you say I didn't –

HICKEY (*soothingly*). Now, Governor. I didn't say anything. You're the only one knows the truth about that.

HOPE *stares at him confusedly.* CORA *continues to play. For a moment there is a pause, broken by* JIMMY TOMORROW, *who speaks with muzzy, self-pitying melancholy out of a sentimental dream.*

JIMMY. Marjorie's favourite song was 'Loch Lomond'. She was beautiful and she played the piano beautifully and she had a beautiful voice. (*With gentle sorrow.*) You were lucky, Harry. Bessie died. But there are more bitter sorrows than losing the woman one loves by the hand of death –

HICKEY (*with an amused wink at* HOPE). Now, listen, Jimmy, you needn't go on. We've all heard that story about how you came

back to Cape Town and found her in the hay with a staff
officer. We know you like to believe that was what started you
on the booze and ruined your life.

JIMMY (*stammers*). I – I'm talking to Harry. Will you kindly keep
out of – (*With a pitiful defiance.*) My life is not ruined!

HICKEY (*ignoring this – with a kidding grin*). But I'll bet when you
admit the truth to yourself, you'll confess you were pretty sick
of her hating you for getting drunk. I'll bet you were really
damned relieved when she gave you such a good excuse.
(JIMMY *stares at him strickenly.* HICKEY *pats him on the back
again – with sincere sympathy.*) I know how it is, Jimmy. I – (*He
stops abruptly and for a second he seems to lose his self-assurance and
become confused.*)

LARRY (*seizing on this with vindictive relish*). Ha! So that's what
happened to you, is it? Your iceman joke finally came home to
roost, did it? (*He grins tauntingly.*) You should have remembered
there's truth in the old superstition that you'd better look out
what you call because in the end it comes to you!

HICKEY (*himself again – grins to* LARRY *kiddingly*). Is that a fact,
Larry? Well, well! Then you'd better watch out how you keep
calling for that old Big Sleep! (LARRY *starts and for a second
looks superstitiously frightened. Abruptly* HICKEY *changes to his
jovial, bustling, master-of-ceremonies manner.*) But what are we
waiting for, boys and girls? Let's start the party rolling! (*He
shouts to the bar.*) Hey, Chuck and Rocky! Bring on the big
surprise! Governor, you sit at the head of the table here.

He makes HARRY *sit down on the chair at the end of the table, right.*

(*To* MARGIE *and* PEARL.) Come on, girls, sit down.

They sit side by side on JIMMY's *right.* HICKEY *bustles down to the
left end of table.*

I'll sit here at the foot.

He sits, with CORA *on his left and* JOE *on her left,* ROCKY *and
CHUCK appear from the bar, each bearing a big tray laden with
schooners of champagne which they start shoving in front of each
member of the party.*

ROCKY (*with forced cheeriness*). Real champagne, bums! Cheer up!
What is dis, a funeral? Jees, mixin' champagne wid Harry's
redeye will knock yuh paralysed! Ain't yuh never satisfied?

He and CHUCK *finish serving out the schooners, grab the last two*

*themselves and sit down in the two vacant chairs remaining near the
table. As they do so,* HICKEY *rises, a schooner in his hand.*

HICKEY (*rapping on the table for order when there is nothing but a
dead silence*). Order! Order, Ladies and Gents! (*He catches*
LARRY's *eyes on the glass in his hand.*) Yes, Larry, I'm going to
drink with you this time. To prove I'm not teetotal because I'm
afraid booze would make me spill my secrets, as you think.
(LARRY *looks sheepish.* HICKEY *chuckles and goes on.*) No, I gave
you the simple truth about that. I don't need booze or anything
else any more. But I want to be sociable and propose a toast in
honour of our old friend, Harry, and drink it with you. (*His
eyes fix on* HUGO, *who is out again, his head on his place. To*
CHUCK, *who is on* HUGO's *left.*) Wake up our demon bomb-
tosser, Chuck. We don't want corpses at this feast.

CHUCK (*gives* HUGO *a shake*). Hey, Hugo, come up for air!
Don't yuh see de champagne?

HUGO *blinks around and giggles foolishly.*

HUGO. Ve vill eat birthday cake and trink champagne beneath
the villow tree! (*He grabs his schooner and takes a greedy gulp –
then sets it back on the table with a grimace of distaste – in a strange,
arrogantly disdainful tone, as if he were rebuking a butler.*) Dis vine
is unfit to trink. It has not properly been iced.

HICKEY (*amusedly*). Always a high-toned swell at heart, eh,
Hugo? God help us poor bums if you'd ever get to telling us
where to get off! You'd have been drinking our blood beneath
those willow trees! (*He chuckles.* HUGO *shrinks back in his chair,
blinking at him, but* HICKEY *is now looking up the table at* HOPE.
*He starts his toast, and as he goes on he becomes more moved and
obviously sincere.*) Here's the toast, Ladies and Gents! Here's to
Harry Hope, who's been a friend in need to every one of us!
Here's to the old Governor, the best sport and the kindest,
biggest-hearted guy in the world! Here's wishing you all the
luck there is, Harry, and long life and happiness! Come on,
everybody! To Harry! Bottoms up!

*They have all caught his sincerity with eager relief. They raise their
schooners with an enthusiastic chorus of* 'Here's how, Harry!'
'Here's luck, Harry!' *etc., and gulp half the wine down,* HICKEY
leading them in this.

HOPE (*deeply moved – his voice husky*). Bejees, thanks, all of you.
Bejees, Hickey, you old son of a bitch, that's white of you!
Bejees, I know you meant it, too.

HICKEY (*moved*). Of course I meant it, Harry, old friend! And I mean it when I say I hope today will be the biggest day in your life, and in the lives of everyone here, the beginning of a new life of peace and contentment where no pipe dreams can ever nag at you again. Here's to that, Harry! (*He drains the remainder of his drink, but this time he drinks alone. In an instant the attitude of everyone has reverted to uneasy, suspicious defensiveness.*)

ROCKY (*growls*). Aw, forget dat bughouse line of bull for a minute, can't yuh?

HICKEY (*sitting down – good-naturedly*). You're right, Rocky, I'm talking too much. It's Harry we want to hear from. Come on, Harry! (*He pounds his schooner on the table.*) Speech! Speech!

They try to recapture their momentary enthusiasm, rap their schooners on the table, call 'Speech,' but there is a hollow ring in it. HOPE *gets to his feet reluctantly, with a forced smile, a smouldering resentment beginning to show in his manner.*

HOPE (*lamely*). Bejees, I'm no good at speeches. All I can say is thanks to everybody again for remembering me on my birthday. (*Bitterness coming out.*) Only don't think because I'm sixty I'll be a bigger damned fool easy mark than ever! No, bejees! Like Hickey says, it's going to be a new day! This dump has got to be run like other dumps, so I can make some money and not just split even. People has got to pay what they owe me! I'm not running a damned orphan asylum for bums and crooks! Nor a God-damned hooker shanty, either! Nor an Old Men's Home for lousy Anarchist tramps that ought to be in jail! I'm sick of being played for a sucker! (*They stare at him with stunned, bewildered hurt. He goes on in a sort of furious desperation, as if he hated himself for every word he said, and yet couldn't stop.*) And don't think you're kidding me right now, either! I know damned well you're giving me the laugh behind my back, thinking to yourselves, The old, lying, pipe-dreaming faker, we've heard his bull about taking a walk around the ward for years, he'll never make it! He's yellow, he ain't got the guts, he's scared he'll find out – (*He glares around at them almost with hatred.*) But I'll show you, bejees! (*He glares at* HICKEY.) I'll show you, too, you son of a bitch of a frying-pan-peddling bastard!

HICKEY (*heartily encouraging*). That's the stuff, Harry! Of course you'll try to show me! That's what I want you to do!

HARRY *glances at him with helpless dread – then drops his eyes and looks furtively around the table. All at once he becomes miserably contrite.*

HOPE (*his voice catching*). Listen, all of you! Bejees, forgive me. I lost my temper! I ain't feeling well! I got a hell of a grouch on! Bejees, you know you're all as welcome here as the flowers in May!

They look at him with eager forgiveness. ROCKY *is the first one who can voice it.*

ROCKY. Aw, sure, Boss, you're always aces wid us, see?

HICKEY (*rises to his feet again. He addresses them now with the simple, convincing sincerity of one making a confession of which he is genuinely ashamed*). Listen, everybody! I know you are sick of my gabbing, but I think this is the spot where I owe it to you to do a little explaining and apologize for some of the rough stuff I've had to pull on you. I know how it must look to you. As if I was a damned busybody who was not only interfering in your private business, but even sicking some of you on to nag at each other. Well, I have to admit that's true, and I'm damned sorry about it. But it simply had to be done! You must believe that! You know old Hickey. I was never one to start trouble. But this time I had to – for your own good! I had to make you help me with each other. I saw I couldn't do what I was after alone. Not in the time at my disposal. I knew when I came here I wouldn't be able to stay with you long. I'm slated to leave on a trip. I saw I'd have to hustle and use every means I could. (*With a joking boastfulness.*) Why, if I had enough time, I'd get a lot of sport out of selling my line of salvation to each of you all by my lonesome. Like it was fun in the old days, when I travelled house to house, to convince some dame, who was sicking the dog on me, her house wouldn't be properly furnished unless she bought another wash boiler. And I could do it with you, all right. I know every one of you, inside and out, by heart. I may have been drunk when I've been here before, but old Hickey could never be so drunk he didn't have to see through people. I mean, everyone except himself. And, finally, he had to see through himself, too. (*He pauses. They stare at him, bitter, uneasy and fascinated. His manner changes to deep earnestness.*) But here's the point to get. I swear I'd never act like I have if I wasn't absolutely sure it will be worth it to you in the end, after you're rid of the damned guilt that makes you lie to yourselves you're something you're not, and the remorse that nags at you and makes you hide behind lousy pipe dreams

about tomorrow. You'll be in a today where there is no
yesterday or tomorrow to worry you. You won't give a damn
what you are any more. I wouldn't say this unless I knew,
Brothers and Sisters. This peace is real! It's a fact! I know!
Because I've got it! Here! Now! Right in front of you! You see
the difference in me! You remember how I used to be! Even
when I had two quarts of rotgut under my belt and joked and
sang 'Sweet Adeline,' I still felt like a guilty skunk. But you can
all see that I don't give a damn about anything now. And I
promise you, by the time this day is over, I'll have every one of
you feeling the same way! (*He pauses. They stare at him
fascinatedly. He adds with a grin.*) I guess that'll be about all from
me, boys and girls – for the present. So let's get on with the
party. (*He starts to sit down.*)

LARRY (*sharply*). Wait! (*Insistently – with a sneer.*) I think it would
help us poor pipe-dreaming sinners along the sawdust trail to
salvation if you told us now what it was happened to you that
converted you to this great peace you've found. (*More and more
with a deliberate, provocative taunting.*) I notice you didn't deny it
when I asked you about the iceman. Did this great revelation of
the evil habit of dreaming about tomorrow come to you after
you found your wife was sick of you?

*While he is speaking the faces of the gang have lighted up vindictively,
as if all at once they saw a chance to revenge themselves. As he finishes,
a chorus of sneering taunts begins, punctuated by nasty, jeering
laughter.*

HOPE. Bejees, you've hit it, Larry! I've noticed he hasn't shown
her picture around this time!

MOSHER. He hasn't got it! The iceman took it away from him!

MARGIE. Jees, look at him! Who could blame her?

PEARL. She must be hard up to fall for an iceman!

CORA. Imagine a sap like him advisin' me and Chuck to git
married!

CHUCK. Yeah! He done so good wid it!

JIMMY. At least I can say Marjorie chose an officer and a
gentleman.

LEWIS. Come to look at you, Hickey, old chap, you've sprouted
horns like a bloody antelope!

WETJOEN. Pigger, py Gott! Like a water buffalo's!

WILLIE (*sings to his Sailor Lad tune*).

> 'Come up,' she cried, 'my iceman lad,
> And you and I'll agree – '

They all join in a jeering chorus, rapping with knuckles or glasses on the table at the indicated spot in the lyric.

> 'And I'll show you the prettiest (*Rap, rap, rap.*)
> That ever you did see!'

A roar of derisive, dirty laughter. But HICKEY *has remained unmoved by all this taunting. He grins good-naturedly, as if he enjoyed the joke at his expense, and joins in the laughter.*

HICKEY. Well, boys and girls, I'm glad to see you getting in good spirits for Harry's party, even if the joke is on me. I admit I asked for it by always pulling that iceman gag in the old days. So laugh all you like. (*He pauses. They do not laugh now. They are again staring at him with baffled uneasiness. He goes on thoughtfully.*) Well, this forces my hand, I guess, your bringing up the subject of Evelyn. I didn't want to tell you yet. It's hardly an appropriate time. I meant to wait until the party was over. But you're getting the wrong idea about poor Evelyn, and I've got to stop that. (*He pauses again. There is a tense stillness in the room. He bows his head a little and says quietly.*) I'm sorry to tell you my dearly beloved wife is dead.

A gasp comes from the stunned company. They look away from him, shocked and miserably ashamed of themselves, except LARRY, *who continues to stare at him.*

LARRY (*aloud to himself with a superstitious shrinking*). Be God, I felt he'd brought the touch of death on him! (*Then suddenly he is even more ashamed of himself than the others and stammers.*) Forgive me, Hickey! I'd like to cut my dirty tongue out!

This releases a chorus of shamefaced mumbles from the crowd. 'Sorry, Hickey.' 'I'm sorry, Hickey.' 'We're sorry, Hickey.'

HICKEY (*looking around at them – in a kindly, reassuring tone*). Now look here, everybody. You mustn't let this be a wet blanket on Harry's party. You're still getting me all wrong. There's no reason – You see, I don't feel any grief. (*They gaze at him startledly. He goes on with convincing sincerity.*) I've got to feel glad, for her sake. Because she's at peace. She's rid of me at last. Hell, I don't have to tell you – you all know what I was like. You can imagine what she went through, married to a no-good cheater and drunk like I was. And there was no way out of it for her. Because she loved me. But now she is at peace like she always longed to be. So why should I feel sad? She wouldn't want me to feel sad. Why, all that Evelyn ever wanted out of life was to make me happy. (*He stops, looking around at them with a simple, gentle frankness.*)

They stare at him in bewildered, incredulous confusion.

Curtain.

ACT THREE

Scene. Bar-room of HARRY HOPE's, *including a part of what had been the back room in Acts One and Two.*

In the right wall are two big windows, with the swinging doors to the street between them. The bar itself is at rear. Behind it is a mirror, covered with white mosquito netting to keep off the flies, and a shelf on which are barrels of cheap whisky with spiggots and a small showcase of bottled goods. At left of the bar is the doorway to the hall. There is a table at left, front of bar-room proper, with four chairs. At right, front, is a small free-lunch counter, facing left, with a space between it and the window for the dealer to stand when he dishes out soup at the noon hour. Over the mirror behind the bar are framed photographs of Richard Croker and Big Tim Sullivan, flanked by framed lithographs of John L. Sullivan and Gentleman Jim Corbett in ring costume.

At left, in what had been the back room, with the dividing curtain drawn, the banquet table of Act Two has been broken up, and the tables are again in the crowded arrangement of Act One. Of these, we see one in the front row with five chairs at left of the bar-room table, another with five chairs at left-rear of it, a third back by the rear wall with five chairs, and finally, at extreme left-front, one with four chairs, partly on and partly off stage, left.

It is around the middle of the morning of HOPE's *birthday, a hot summer day. There is sunlight in the street outside, but it does not hit the windows and the light in the back-room section is dim.*

JOE MOTT *is moving around, a box of sawdust under his arm, strewing it over the floor. His manner is sullen, his face set in gloom. He ignores everyone. As the scene progresses, he finishes his sawdusting job, goes behind the lunch counter and cuts loaves of bread.* ROCKY *is behind the bar, wiping it, washing glasses, etc. He wears his working clothes, sleeves rolled up. He looks sleepy, irritable and worried. At the bar-room table, front,* LARRY *sits in a chair, facing right-front. He has no drink in front of him. He stares ahead, deep in harried thought. On his right, in a chair facing right,* HUGO *sits sprawled forward, arms and head on the table as usual, a whisky glass beside his limp hand. At rear of the front table at left of them, in a chair facing left,* PARRITT *is sitting. He is staring in front of him in a tense, strained immobility.*

As the curtain rises, ROCKY *finishes his work behind the bar. He comes forward and drops wearily in the chair at right of* LARRY'*s table, facing left.*

ROCKY. Nuttin' now till de noon rush from de Market. I'm goin' to rest my fanny. (*Irritably.*) If I ain't a sap to let Chuck kid me into workin' his time so's he can take de mornin' off. But I got sick of arguin' wid 'im. I says, 'Aw right, git married! What's it to me?' Hickey's got de bot' of dem bugs. (*Bitterly.*) Some party last night, huh? Jees, what a funeral! It was jinxed from de start, but his tellin' about his wife croakin' put de KO on it.

LARRY. Yes, it turned out it wasn't a birthday feast but a wake!

ROCKY. Him promisin' he'd cut out de bughouse bull about peace – and den he went on talkin' and talkin' like he couldn't stop! And all de gang sneakin' upstairs, leavin' free booze and eats like dey was poison! It didn't do dem no good if dey thought dey'd shake him. He's been hoppin' from room to room all night. Yuh can't stop him. He's got his Reform Wave goin' strong dis mornin'! Did yuh notice him drag Jimmy out de foist ting to get his laundry and his clothes pressed so he wouldn't have no excuse? And he give Willie de dough to buy his stuff back from Solly's. And all de rest been brushin' and shavin' demselves wid de shakes –

LARRY (*defiantly*). He didn't come to my room! He's afraid I might ask him a few questions.

ROCKY (*scornfully*). Yeah? It don't look to me he's scared of yuh. I'd say you was scared of him.

LARRY (*stung*). You'd lie, then!

PARRITT (*jerks round to look at* LARRY – *sneeringly*). Don't let him kid you, Rocky. He had his door locked. I couldn't get in, either.

ROCKY. Yeah, who d'yuh tink yuh're kiddin', Larry? He's showed you up, aw right. Like he says, if yuh was so anxious to croak, why wouldn't yuh hop off your fire escape long ago?

LARRY (*defiantly*). Because it'd be a coward's quitting, that's why!

PARRITT. He's all quitter, Rocky. He's a yellow old faker!

LARRY (*turns on him*). You lying punk! Remember what I warned you – !

ROCKY (*scowls at* PARRITT). Yeah, keep outta dis, you! Where d'yuh get a licence to butt in? Shall I give him de bum's rush, Larry? If you don't want him around, nobody else don't.

LARRY (*forcing an indifferent tone*). No. Let him stay. I don't mind him. He's nothing to me.

ROCKY *shrugs his shoulders and yawns sleepily.*

PARRITT. You're right, I have nowhere to go now. You're the only one in the world I can turn to.

ROCKY (*drowsily*). Yuh're a soft old sap, Larry. He's a no-good louse like Hickey. He don't belong. (*He yawns.*) I'm all in. Not a wink of sleep. Can't keep my peepers open. (*His eyes close and his head nods.*)

PARRITT *gives him a glance and then gets up and slinks over to slide into the chair on* LARRY's *left, between him and* ROCKY. LARRY *shrinks away, but determinedly ignores him.*

PARRITT (*bending towards him – in a low, ingratiating, apologetic voice*). I'm sorry for riding you, Larry. But you get my goat when you act as if you didn't care a damn what happened to me, and keep your door locked so I can't talk to you. (*Then hopefully.*) But that was to keep Hickey out, wasn't it? I don't blame you. I'm getting to hate him. I'm getting more and more scared of him. Especially since he told us his wife was dead. It's that queer feeling he gives me that I'm mixed up with him some way. I don't know why, but it started me thinking about Mother – as if she was dead. (*With a strange undercurrent of something like satisfaction in his pitying tone.*) I suppose she might as well be. Inside herself, I mean. It must kill her when she thinks of me – I know she doesn't want to, but she can't help it. After all, I'm her only kid. She used to spoil me and made a pet of me. Once in a great while, I mean. When she remembered me. As if she wanted to make up for something. As if she felt guilty. So she must have loved me a little, even if she never let it interfere with her freedom. (*With a strange pathetic wistfulness.*) Do you know, Larry, I once had a sneaking suspicion that maybe, if the truth was known, you were my father.

LARRY (*violently*). You damned fool! Who put that insane idea in your head? You know it's a lie! Anyone in the Coast crowd could tell you I never laid eyes on your mother till after you were born.

PARRITT. Well, I'd hardly ask them, would I? I know you're right, though, because I asked her. She brought me up to be frank and ask her anything, and she'd always tell me the truth.

(*Abruptly.*) But I was talking about how she must feel now about me. My getting through with the Movement. She'll never forgive that. The Movement is her life. And it must be the final knockout for her if she knows I was the one who sold –

LARRY. Shut up, damn you!

PARRITT. It'll kill her. And I'm sure she knows it must have been me. (*Suddenly with desperate urgency.*) But I never thought the cops would get her! You've got to believe that! You've got to see what my only reason was! I'll admit what I told you last night was a lie – that bunk about getting patriotic and my duty to my country. But here's the true reason, Larry – the only reason! It was just for money! I got stuck on a whore and wanted dough to blow in on her and have a good time! That's all I did it for! Just money! Honest! (*He has the terrible grotesque air, in confessing his sordid baseness, of one who gives an excuse which exonerates him from any real guilt.*)

LARRY (*grabs him by the shoulder and shakes him*). God damn you, shut up! What the hell is it to me?

ROCKY *starts awake.*

ROCKY. What's comin' off here?

LARRY (*controlling himself*). Nothing. This gabby young punk was talking my ear off, that's all. He's a worse pest than Hickey.

ROCKY (*drowsily*). Yeah, Hickey – Say, listen, what d'yuh mean about him bein' scared you'd ask him questions? What questions?

LARRY. Well, I feel he's hiding something. You notice he didn't say what his wife died of.

ROCKY (*rebukingly*). Aw, lay off dat. De poor guy – What are yuh gettin' at, anyway? Yuh don't tink it's just a gag of his?

LARRY. I don't. I'm damned sure he's brought death here with him. I feel the cold touch of it on him.

ROCKY. Aw, bunk! You got croakin' on de brain, Old Cemetery. (*Suddenly* ROCKY's *eyes widen.*) Say! D'yuh mean yuh tink she committed suicide, 'count of his cheatin' or someting?

LARRY (*grimly*). It wouldn't surprise me. I'd be the last to blame her.

ROCKY (*scornfully*). But dat's crazy! Jees, if she'd done dat, he wouldn't tell us he was glad about it, would he? He ain't dat big a bastard.

PARRITT (*speaks up from his own preoccupation – strangely*). You know better than that, Larry. You know she'd never commit suicide. She's like you. She'll hang on to life even when there's nothing left but –

LARRY (*stung – turns on him viciously*). And how about you? Be God, if you had any guts or decency – ! (*He stops guiltily.*)

PARRITT (*sneeringly*). I'd take that hop off your fire escape you're too yellow to take, I suppose?

LARRY (*as if to himself*). No! Who am I to judge? I'm done with judging.

PARRITT (*tauntingly*). Yes, I suppose you'd like that, wouldn't you?

ROCKY (*irritably mystified*). What de hell's all dis about? (*To PARRITT.*) What d'you know about Hickey's wife? How d'yuh know she didn't – ?

LARRY (*with forced belittling casualness*). He doesn't. Hickey's addled the little brains he's got. Shove him back to his own table, Rocky. I'm sick of him.

ROCKY (*to PARRITT, threateningly*). Yuh heard Larry? I'd like an excuse to give yuh a good punch in de snoot. So move quick!

PARRITT (*gets up – to LARRY*). If you think moving to another table will get rid of me! (*He moves away – then adds with bitter reproach.*) Gee, Larry, that's a hell of a way to treat me, when I've trusted you and I need your help. (*He sits down in his old place and sinks into a wounded, self-pitying brooding.*)

ROCKY (*going back to his train of thought*). Jees, if she committed suicide, yuh got to feel sorry for Hickey, huh? Yuh can understand how he'd go bughouse and not be responsible for all de crazy stunts he's stagin' here. (*Then puzzledly.*) But how can yuh be sorry for him when he says he's glad she croaked, and yuh can tell he means it? (*With weary exasperation.*) Aw, nuts! I don't get nowhere tryin' to figger his game. (*His face hardening.*) But I know dis. He better lay off me and my stable! (*He pauses – then sighs.*) Jees, Larry, what a night dem two pigs give me! When de party went dead, dey pinched a coupla bottles and brung dem up deir room and got stinko. I don't get a wink of sleep, see? Just as I'd drop off on a chair here, dey'd come down lookin' for trouble. Or else dey'd raise hell upstairs, laughin' and singin', so I'd get scared dey'd get de joint pinched and go up to tell dem to can de noise. And every time dey'd crawl my frame wid de same old argument. Dey'd say, 'So yuh agreed wid Hickey, do yuh, yuh dirty little Ginny? We're whores, are we? Well, we agree wid Hickey about you, see! Yuh're nuttin' but a lousy pimp!' Den I'd slap dem. Not beat 'em up, like a pimp would. Just slap dem. But it don't do no good. Dey'd keep at it over and over. Jees, I get de earache just thinkin' of it! 'Listen,' dey'd say, 'if we're whores we gotta right to have a reg'lar pimp and not stand for no punk imitation! We're sick of wearin' out our dogs poundin' sidewalks for a double-crossin' bartender, when all de thanks we get is he looks down on us. We'll find a guy who really needs us to take care of him and ain't ashamed of it. Don't expect us to work tonight, 'cause we won't, see? Not if de streets was blocked wid sailors! We're goin' on strike and yuh can like it or lump it!' (*He shakes his head.*) Whores goin' on strike! Can yuh tie dat? (*Going on with his story.*) Dey says, 'We're takin' a holiday. We're goin' to beat it down to Coney Island and shoot the chutes and maybe we'll come back and maybe we won't. And you can go to hell!' So dey put on deir lids and beat it, de bot' of dem stinko.

He sighs dejectedly. He seems grotesquely like a harried family man, henpecked and browbeaten by a nagging wife. LARRY is deep in his own bitter preoccupation and hasn't listened to him. CHUCK enters from the hall at rear. He has his straw hat with the gaudy band in his hand and wears a Sunday-best blue suit with a high stiff collar. He looks sleepy, hot uncomfortable and grouchy.

CHUCK (*glumly*). Hey, Rocky. Cora wants a sherry flip. For her noives.

ROCKY (*turns indignantly*). Sherry flip! Christ, she don't need nuttin' for her noive! What's she tink dis is, de Waldorf?

CHUCK. Yeah, I told her, what would we use for sherry, and dere wasn't no egg unless she laid one. She says, 'Is dere a law yuh can't go out and buy de makings, yuh big tramp?' (*Resentfully puts his straw hat on his head at a defiant tilt.*) To hell wid her! She'll drink booze or nuttin'! (*He goes behind the bar to draw a glass of whisky from a barrel.*)

ROCKY (*sarcastically*). Jees, a guy oughta give his bride anything she wants on de weddin' day, I should tink!

As CHUCK comes from behind the bar, ROCKY surveys him derisively.

Pipe de bridegroom, Larry! All dolled up for de killin'!

LARRY *pays no attention.*

CHUCK. Aw, shut up!

ROCKY. One week on dat farm in Joisey, dat's what I give yuh! Yuh'll come runnin' in here some night yellin' for a shot of booze 'cause de crickets is after yuh! (*Disgustedly.*) Jees, Chuck, dat louse Hickey's coitinly made a prize coupla suckers outa youse.

CHUCK (*unguardedly*). Yeah. I'd like to give him one sock in de puss – just one! (*Then angrily.*) Aw, can dat! What's he got to do wid it? Ain't we always said we was goin' to? So we're goin' to, see? And don't give me no argument! (*He stares at ROCKY truculently. But ROCKY only shrugs his shoulders with weary disgust and CHUCK subsides into complaining gloom.*) If on'y Cora'd cut out de beefin'. She don't gimme a minute's rest all night. De same old stuff over and over! Do I really want to marry her? I says, 'Sure, Baby, why not?' She says, 'Yeah, but after a week yuh'll be tinkin' what a sap you was. Yuh'll make dat an excuse to go off on a periodical, and den I'll be tied for life to a no-good soak, and de foist ting I know yuh'll have me out hustlin' again, your own wife!' Den she'd bust out cryin', and I'd get sore. 'Yuh're a liar,' I'd say. 'I aint never taken your dough 'cept when I was drunk and not workin'!' 'Yeah,' she'd say, 'and how long will yuh stay sober now? Don't tink yuh can kid me wid dat water wagon bull! I've heard it too often.' Dat'd make me sore and I'd say, 'Don't call me a liar. But I wish I was drunk right now, because if I was, yuh wouldn't be keepin' me awake all night beefin'. If yuh opened your yap, I'd knock de stuffin' outa yuh!' Den she'd yell, 'Dat's a sweet way to talk to de goil yuh're goin' to marry. (*He sighs explosively.*) Jees, she's got me hangin' on de ropes! (*He glances with vengeful yearning at the drink of whisky in his hand.*) Jees, would I like to get a quart of dis redeye under my belt!

ROCKY. Well, why de hell don't yuh?

CHUCK (*instantly suspicious and angry*). Sure! You'd like dat, wouldn't yuh? I'm wise to you! Yuh don't wanta see me get married and settle down like a reg'lar guy! Yuh'd like me to stay paralysed all de time, so's I'd be like you, a lousy pimp!

ROCKY (*springs to his feet, his face hardened viciously*). Listen! I don't take dat even from you, see!

CHUCK (*puts his drink on the bar and clenches his fists*). Yeah?

Wanta make sometin' of it? (*Jeeringly.*) Don't make me laugh! I can lick ten of youse wid one mit!

ROCKY (*reaching for his hip pocket*). Not wid lead in your belly, yuh won't!

JOE (*has stopped cutting when the quarrel started – expostulating*). Hey, you, Rocky and Chuck! Cut it out! You's ole friends! Don't let dat Hickey make you crazy!

CHUCK (*turns on him*). Keep outa our business, yuh black bastard!

ROCKY (*like CHUCK, turns on JOE, as if their own quarrel was forgotten and they became natural allies against an alien*). Stay where yuh belong, yuh doity nigger!

JOE (*snarling with rage, springs from behind the lunch counter with the bread knife in his hand*). You white sons of bitches! I'll rip your guts out!

CHUCK *snatches a whisky bottle from the bar and raises it above his head to hurl at* JOE. ROCKY *jerks a short-barrelled, nickel-plated revolver from his hip pocket. At this moment* LARRY *pounds on the table with his fist and bursts into a sardonic laugh.*

LARRY. That's it! Murder each other, you damned loons, with Hickey's blessing! Didn't I tell you he'd brought death with him:

His interruption startles them. They pause to stare at him, their fighting fury suddenly dies out and they appear deflated and sheepish.

ROCKY (*to JOE*). Aw right, you. Leggo dat shiv and I'll put dis gat away.

JOE *sullenly goes back behind the counter and slaps the knife on top of it.* ROCKY *slips the revolver back in his pocket.* CHUCK *lowers the bottle to the bar.* HUGO, *who has awakened and raised his head when* LARRY *pounded on the table, now giggles foolishly.*

HUGO. Hello, leedle peoples. Neffer mind! Soon you vill eat hot dogs beneath the villow trees and trink free vine – (*Abruptly in a haughty fastidious tone.*) The champagne vas not properly iced. (*With guttural anger.*) Gottamned liar, Hickey! Does that prove I vant to be aristocrat? I love only the proletariat! I vill lead them! I vill be like a Gott to them! They vill be my slaves! (*He stops in bewildered self-amazement – to* LARRY *appealingly.*) I am very trunk, no, Larry? I talk foolishness. I am so trunk, Larry, old friend, am I not, I don't know vhat I say?

LARRY (*pityingly*). You're raving drunk, Hugo. I've never seen you so paralysed. Lay your head down now and sleep it off.

HUGO (*gratefully*). Yes. I should sleep. I am too crazy trunk. (*He puts his head on his arms and closes his eyes.*)

JOE (*behind the lunch counter – brooding superstitiously*). You's right, Larry. Bad luck come in de door when Hickey come. I's an ole gamblin' man and I knows bad luck when I feels it! (*Then defiantly.*) But it's white man's bad luck. He can't jinx me! (*He comes from behind the counter and goes to the bar – addressing* ROCKY *stiffly.*) De bread's cut and I's finished my job. Do I get de drink I's earned?

ROCKY *gives him a hostile look but shoves a bottle and glass at him.* JOE *pours a brimful drink – sullenly.*

I's finished wid dis dump for keeps. (*He takes a key from his pocket and slaps it on the bar.*) Here's de key to my room. I ain't comin' back. I's goin' to my own folks where I belong. I don't stay where I's not wanted. I's sick and tired of messin' round wid white men. (*He gulps down his drink – then looking around defiantly he deliberately throws his whisky glass on the floor and smashes it.*)

ROCKY. Hey! What de hell – !

JOE (*with a sneering dignity*). I's on'y savin' you de trouble, White Boy. Now you don't have to break it, soon's my back's turned, so's no white man kick about drinkin' from de same glass. (*He walks stiffly to the street door – then turns for a parting shot – boastfully.*) I's tired of loafin' 'round wid a lot of bums. I's a gamblin' man. I's gonna get in a big crap game and win me a big bank-roll. Den I'll get de okay to open up my old gamblin' house for coloured men. Den maybe I comes back here sometime to see de bums. Maybe I throw a twenty-dollar bill on de bar and say, 'Drink it up,' and listen when dey all pat me on de back and say, 'Joe, you sure is white.' But I'll say, 'No, I'm black and my dough is black man's dough, and you's proud to drink wid me or you don't get no drink!' Or maybe I just says, 'You can all go to hell. I don't lower myself drinkin' wid no white trash!' (*He opens the door to go out – then turns again.*) And dat ain't no pipe dream! I'll git de money for my stake today, somehow, somewheres! If I has to borrow a gun and stick up some white man, I gets it! You wait and see! (*He swaggers out through the swinging doors.*)

CHUCK (*angrily*). Can yuh beat de noive of dat dinge! Jees, if I wasn't dressed up, I'd go out and mop up de street wid him!

ROCKY. Aw, let him go, de poor old dope! Him and his gamblin' house! He'll be back tonight askin' Harry for his room and bummin' me for a ball. (*Vengefully.*) Den I'll be de one to smash de glass. I'll loin him his place!

The swinging doors are pushed open and WILLIE OBAN *enters from the street. He is shaved and wears an expensive, well-cut suit, good shoes and clean linen. He is absolutely sober, but his face is sick, and his nerves in a shocking state of shakes.*

CHUCK. Another guy all dolled up! Got your clothes from Solly's, huh Willie? (*Derisively.*) Now yuh can sell dem back to him again tomorrow.

WILLIE (*stiffly*). No, I – I'm through with that stuff. Never again. (*He comes to the bar.*)

ROCKY (*sympathetically*). Yuh look sick, Willie. Take a ball to pick yuh up. (*He pushes a bottle toward him.*)

WILLIE (*eyes the bottle yearningly but shakes his head – determinedly*). No, thanks. The only way to stop is to stop. I'd have no chance if I went to the DA's office smelling of booze.

CHUCK. Yuh're really goin' dere?

WILLIE (*stiffly*). I said I was, didn't I? I just came back here to rest a few minutes, not because I needed any booze. I'll show that cheap drummer I don't have to have any Dutch courage – (*Guiltily.*) But he's been very kind and generous staking me. He can't help his insulting manner, I suppose. (*He turns away from the bar.*) My legs are a bit shaky yet. I better sit down a while.

He goes back and sits at the left of the second table, facing PARRITT, *who gives him a scowling, suspicious glance and then ignores him.* ROCKY *looks at* CHUCK *and taps his head disgustedly.* CAPTAIN LEWIS *appears in the doorway from the hall.*

CHUCK (*mutters*). Here's anudder one.

LEWIS *looks spruce and clean-shaven. His ancient tweed suit has been brushed and his frayed linen is clean. His manner is full of a forced, jaunty self-assurance. But he is sick and beset by katzenjammer.*

LEWIS. Good morning, gentlemen all. (*He passes along the front of bar to look out in the street.*) A jolly fine morning, too. (*He turns back to the bar.*) An eye-opener? I think not. Not required, Rocky, old chum. Feel extremely fit, as a matter of fact. Though can't say I slept much, thanks to that interfering ass, Hickey and that stupid bounder of a Boer. (*His face hardens.*) I've had about all I can take from that fellow. It's my own fault of course, for allowing a brute of a Dutch farmer to become familiar. Well, it's come to a parting of the ways now, and good riddance. Which reminds me, here's my key. (*He puts it on the bar.*) I shan't be coming back. Sorry to be leaving good old Harry and the rest of you, of course, but I can't continue to live under the same roof with that fellow.

He stops, stiffening into hostility as WETJOEN *enters from the hall, and pointedly turns his back on him.* WETJOEN *glares at him sneeringly. He, too, has made an effort to spruce up his appearance, and his bearing has a forced swagger of conscious physical strength. Behind this, he is sick and feebly holding his booze-sodden body together.*

ROCKY (*to* LEWIS – *disgustedly putting the key on the shelf in back of the bar*). So Hickey's kidded the pants offa you, too? Yuh tink yuh're leavin' here, huh?

WETJOEN (*jeeringly*). Ja! Dot's vhat he kids himself.

LEWIS (*ignores him – airily*). Yes, I'm leaving, Rocky. But that ass, Hickey, has nothing to do with it. Been thinking things over. Time I turned over a new leaf, and all that.

WETJOEN. He's going to get a job! Dot's vhat he says!

ROCKY. What at, for Chris' sake?

LEWIS (*keeping his airy manner*). Oh, anything. I mean, not manual labour, naturally, but anything that calls for a bit of brains and education. However humble. Beggars can't be choosers. I'll see a pal of mine at the Consulate. He promised any time I felt an energetic fit he'd get me a post with the Cunard – clerk in the office or something of the kind.

WETJOEN. Ja! At Limey Consulate they promise anything to get rid of him vhen he comes there tronk! They're scared to call the police and have him pinched because it vould scandal in the papers make about a Limey officer and chentleman!

LEWIS. As a matter of fact, Rocky, I only wish a post temporarily. Means to an end, you know. Save up enough for a first-class passage home, that's the bright idea.

WETJOEN. He's sailing back to home, sveet home! Dot's biggest pipe dream of all. What leetle brain the poor Limey has left, dot isn't in whisky pickled, Hickey has made crazy!

LEWIS's *fists clench, but he manages to ignore this.*

CHUCK (*feels sorry for* LEWIS *and turns on* WETJOEN –

sarcastically). Hickey ain't made no sucker outa you, huh? You're too foxy, huh? But I'll bet you tink yuh're goin' out and land a job, too.

WETJOEN (*bristles*). I am, ja. For me, it is easy. Because I put on no airs of chentleman. I am not ashamed to vork vith my hands. I vas a farmer before the war ven ploody Limey thieves steel my country. (*Boastfully*.) Anyone I ask for job can see vith one look I have the great strength to do work of ten ordinary mens.

LEWIS (sneeringly). Yes, Chuck, you remember he gave a demonstration of his extraordinary muscles last night when he helped to move the piano.

CHUCK. Yuh couldn't even hold up your corner. It was your fault de damned box almost fell down de stairs.

WETJOEN. My hands vas sweaty! Could I help dot my hands slip? I could de whole veight of it lift! In old days in Transvaal, I lift loaded oxcart by the axle! So vhy shouldn't I get job? Dot longshoreman boss, Dan, he tell me any time I like, he take me on. And Benny from de Market he promise me same.

LEWIS. You remember, Rocky, it was one of those rare occasions when the Boer that walks like a man – spelled with a double o, by the way – was buying drinks and Dan and Benny were stony. They'd bloody well have promised him the moon

ROCKY. Yeah, yuh big boob, dem boids was on'y kiddin' yuh.

WETJOEN (*angrily*). Dot's lie! You vill see dis morning I get job! I'll show dot bloody Limey chentleman, and dot liar, Hickey! And I need vork only leetle vhile to save money for my passage home. I need not much money because I am not ashamed to travel steerage. I don't put on first-cabin airs! (*Tauntingly,*) Und *I can* go home to my country! Vhen I get there, they vill let *me* come in!

LEWIS (*grows rigid – his voice trembling with repressed anger*). There was a rumour in South Africa, Rocky, that a certain Boer officer – if you call the leaders of a rabble of farmers officers – kept advising Cronje to retreat and not stand and fight –

WETJOEN. And I vas right! I vas right! He got surrounded at Poardeberg! He had to surrender!

LEWIS (*ignoring him*). Good strategy, no doubt, but a suspicion grew afterwards into a conviction among the Boers that the officer's caution was prompted by a desire to make his personal escape. His countrymen felt extremely savage about it, and his family disowned him. So I imagine there would be no welcoming committee waiting on the dock, nor delighted relatives making the veldt ring with their happy cries –

WETJOEN (*with guilty rage*). All lies! You Gottamned Limey – (*Trying to control himself and copy* LEWIS's *manner.*) I also haf heard rumours of a Limey officer who, after the war, lost all his money gambling vhen he vas tronk. But they found out it was regiment money, too, he lost –

LEWIS (*loses his control and starts for him*). You bloody Dutch scum!

ROCKY (*leans over the bar and stops* LEWIS *with a straight-arm swipe on the chest*). Cut it out!

At the same moment CHUCK *grabs* WETJOEN *and yanks him back.*

WETJOEN (*struggling*). Let him come! I saw them come before – at Modder River, Magersfontein, Spion Kopje – waving their silly swords, so afraid they couldn't show off how brave they vas! and I kill them vith my rifle so easy! (*Vindictively.*) Listen to me, you Cecil! Often vhen I am tronk and kidding you I say I am sorry I missed you, but now, py Gott, I am sober, and I don't joke, and I say it!

LARRY (*gives a sardonic guffaw – with his comically crazy, intense whisper*). Be God, you can't say Hickey hasn't the miraculous touch to raise the dead, when he can start the Boer War raging again!

This interruption acts like a cold douche on LEWIS *and* WETJOEN. *They subside, and* ROCKY *and* CHUCK *let go of them.* LEWIS *turns his back on the Boer.*

LEWIS (*attempting a return of his jaunty manner, as if nothing had happened*). Well, time I was on my merry way to see my chap at the Consulate. The early bird catches the job, what? Goodbye and good luck, Rocky, and everyone. (*He starts for the street door.*)

WETJOEN. Py Gott, if dot Limey can go, I can go!

He hurries after LEWIS. *But* LEWIS, *his hand about to push the swinging doors open, hesitates, as though struck by a sudden paralysis of the will, and* WETJOEN *has to jerk back to avoid bumping into him. For a second they stand there, one behind the other, staring over the swinging doors into the street.*

ROCKY. Well, why don't yuh beat it?

LEWIS (*guiltily casual*). Eh? Oh, just happened to think. Hardly
the decent thing to pop off without saying goodbye to old
Harry. One of the best, Harry. And good old Jimmy, too. They
ought to be down any moment. (*He pretends to notice* WETJOEN
*for the first time and steps away from the door – apologizing as to a
stranger.*) Sorry. I seem to be blocking your way out.

WETJOEN (*stiffly*). No. I vait to say goodbye to Harry and
Jimmy, too.

*He goes to right of door behind the lunch counter and looks through the
window, his back to the room.* LEWIS *takes up a similar stand at the
window on the left of door.*

CHUCK. Jees, can yuh beat dem simps! (*He picks up* CORA's
drink at the end of the bar.) Hell, I'd forgot Cora. She'll be trowin'
a fit. (*He goes into the hall with the drink.*)

ROCKY (*looks after him disgustedly*). Dat's right, wait on her and
spoil her, yuh poor sap! (*He shakes his head and begins to wipe the
bar mechanically.*)

WILLIE (*is regarding* PARRITT *across the table from him with an
eager, calculating eye. He leans over and speaks in a low confidential
tone*). Look here, Parritt. I'd like to have a talk with you.

PARRITT (*starts – scowling defensively*). What about?

WILLIE (*his manner becoming his idea of a crafty criminal lawyer's*).
About the trouble you're in. Oh, I know. You don't admit it.
You're quite right. That's my advice. Deny everything. Keep
your mouth shut. Make no statements whatever without first
consulting your attorney.

PARRITT. Say! What the hell – ?

WILLIE. But you can trust me. I'm a lawyer, and it's just
occurred to me you and I ought to co-operate. Of course I'm
going to see the DA this morning about a job on his staff. But
that may take time. There may not be an immediate opening.
Meanwhile it would be a good idea for me to take a case or
two, on my own, and prove my brilliant record in law school
was no flash in the pan. So why not retain me as your attorney?

PARRITT. You're crazy! What do I want with a lawyer?

WILLIE. That's right. Don't admit anything. But you can trust
me, so let's not beat about the bush. You got in trouble out on
the Coast, eh? And now you're hiding out. Any fool can spot
that. (*Lowering his voice still more.*) You feel safe here, and maybe

you are, for a while. But remember, they get you in the end. I know from my father's experience. No one could have felt safer than he did. When anyone mentioned the law to him, he nearly died laughing. But –

PARRITT. You crazy mutt! (*Turning to* LARRY *with a strained laugh.*) Did you get that, Larry? This damned fool thinks the cops are after me!

LARRY (*bursts out with his true reaction before he thinks to ignore him*). I wish to God they were! And so should you, if you had the honour of a louse!

PARRITT *stares into his eyes guiltily for a second. Then he smiles sneeringly.*

PARRITT. And you're the guy who kids himself he's through with the Movement! You old lying faker, you're still in love with it!

LARRY *ignores him again now.*

WILLIE (*disappointedly*). Then you're not in trouble, Parritt? I was hoping – But never mind. No offence meant. Forget it.

PARRITT (*condescendingly – his eyes on* LARRY). Sure. That's all right, Willie. I'm not sore at you. It's that damned old faker that gets my goat. (*He slips out of his chair and goes quietly over to sit in the chair beside* LARRY *he had occupied before – in a low, insinuating, intimate tone.*) I think I understand, Larry. It's really Mother you still love – isn't it? – in spite of the dirty deal she gave you. But hell, what did you expect? She was never true to anyone but herself and the Movement. But I understand how you can't help still feeling – because I still love her, too. (*Pleading in a strained, desperate tone.*) You know I do, don't you? You must! So you see I couldn't have expected they'd catch her! You've got to believe me that I sold them out just to get a few lousy dollars to blow in on a whore. No other reason, honest! There couldn't possibly be any other reason! (*Again he has a strange air of exonerating himself from guilt by this shameless confession.*)

LARRY (*trying not to listen, has listened with increasing tension*). For the love of Christ will you leave me in peace! I've told you you can't make me judge you! But if you don't keep still, you'll be saying something soon that will make you vomit your own soul like a drink of nickel rotgut that won't stay down! (*He pushes back his chair and springs to his feet.*) To hell with you! (*He goes to the bar.*)

PARRITT (*jumps up and starts to follow him – desperately*). Don't go, Larry! You've got to help me!

But LARRY *is at the bar, back turned, and* ROCKY *is scowling at him. He stops, shrinking back into himself helplessly, and turns away. He goes to the table where he had been before, and this time he takes the chair at rear facing directly front. He puts his elbows on the table, holding his head in his hands as if he had a splitting headache.*

LARRY. Set 'em up, Rocky. I swore I'd have no more drinks on Hickey, if I died of drought, but I've changed my mind! Be God, he owed it to me, and I'd get blind to the world now if it was the Iceman of Death himself treating! (*He stops, startledly, a superstitious awe coming into his face.*) What made me say that, I wonder. (*With a sardonic laugh.*) Well, be God, it fits, for Death was the Iceman Hickey called to his home.

ROCKY. Aw, forget dat iceman gag! De poor dame is dead. (*Pushing a bottle and glass at* LARRY.) Gwan and get paralysed! I'll be glad to see one bum in dis dump act natural.

LARRY *downs a drink and pours another.* ED MOSHER *appears in the doorway from the hall. The same change which is apparent in the manner and appearance of the others shows in him. He is sick, his nerves are shattered, his eyes are apprehensive, but he, too, puts on an exaggeratedly self-confident bearing. He saunters to the bar between* LARRY *and the street entrance.*

MOSHER. Morning, Rocky. Hello, Larry. Glad to see Brother Hickey hasn't corrupted you to temperance. I wouldn't mind a shot myself. (*As* ROCKY *shoves a bottle toward him he shakes his head.*) But I remember the only breath-killer in this dump is coffee beans. The boss would never fall for that. No man can run a circus successfully who believes guys chew coffee beans because they like them. (*He pushes the bottle away.*) No, much as I need one after the hell of a night I've had – (*He scowls.*) That drummer son of a drummer! I had to lock him out. But I could hear him through the wall doing his spiel to someone all night long. Still at it with Jimmy and Harry when I came down just now. But the hardest to take was that flannel-mouth, flatfoot Mick trying to tell me where I got off! I had to lock him out, too.

As he says this, MCGLOIN *comes in the doorway from the hall. The change in his appearance and manner is identical with that of* MOSHER *and the others.*

MCGLOIN. He's a liar, Rocky! It was me locked him out!

MOSHER *starts to flare up – then ignores him. They turn their backs on each other.* MCGLOIN *starts into the back-room section.*

WILLIE. Come and sit here, Mac. You're just the man I want to see. If I'm to take your case, we ought to have a talk before we leave.

MCGLOIN (*contemptuously*). We'll have no talk. You damned fool, do you think I'd have your father's son for my lawyer? They'd take one look at you and bounce us both out on our necks! (WILLIE *winces and shrinks down in his chair.* MCGLOIN *goes to the first table beyond him and sits with his back to the bar.*) I don't need a lawyer, anyway. To hell with the law! All I've got to do is see the right ones and get them to pass the word. They will, too. They know I was framed. And once they've passed the word, it's as good as done, law or no law.

MOSHER. God, I'm glad I'm leaving this madhouse! (*He pulls his key from his pocket and slaps it on the bar.*) Here's my key, Rocky.

MCGLOIN (*pulls his from his pocket*). And here's mine. (*He tosses it to* ROCKY.) I'd rather sleep in the gutter than pass another night under the same roof with that loon, Hickey, and a lying circus grifter! (*He adds darkly.*) And if that hat fits anyone here, let him put it on!

MOSHER *turns toward him furiously but* ROCKY *leans over the bar and grabs his arm.*

ROCKY. Nix! Take it easy! (MOSHER *subsides.* ROCKY *tosses the keys on the shelf – disgustedly.*) You boids gimme a pain. It'd soive you right if I wouldn't give de keys back to yuh tonight.

They both turn on him resentfully, but there is an interruption as CORA *appears in the doorway from the hall with* CHUCK *behind her. She is drunk, dressed in her gaudy best, her face plastered with rouge and mascara, her hair a bit dishevelled, her hat on anyhow.*

CORA (*comes a few steps inside the bar – with a strained bright giggle*). Hello, everybody! Here we go! Hickey just told us, ain't it time we beat it, if we're really goin'. So we're showin' de bastard, ain't we. Honey? He's comin' right down wid Harry and Jimmy. Jees, dem two look like dey was goin' to de electric chair! (*With frightened anger.*) If I had to listen to any more of Hickey's bunk, I'd brain him. (*She puts her hand on* CHUCK's *arm.*) Come on, Honey. Let's get started before he comes down.

CHUCK (*sullenly*). Sure, anything yuh say, Baby.

CORA (*turns on him truculently*). Yeah? Well, I say we stop at de foist reg'lar dump and yuh gotta blow me to a sherry flip – or four or five, if I want 'em! – or all bets is off!

CHUCK. Aw, yuh got a fine bun on now!

CORA. Cheap skate! I know what's eatin' you. Tightwad! Well, use my dough, den, if yuh're so stingy. Yuh'll grab it all, anyway, right after de ceremony. I know you! (*She hikes her skirt up and reaches inside the top of her stocking.*) Here, yuh big tramp!

CHUCK (*knocks her hand away – angrily*). Keep your lousy dough! And don't show off your legs to dese bums when yuh're goin' to be married, if yuh don't want a sock in de puss!

CORA (*pleased – meekly*). Aw right, Honey. (*Looking around with a foolish laugh.*) Say, why don't all you barflies come to de weddin'? (*But they are all sunk in their own apprehensions and ignore her. She hesitates, miserably uncertain.*) Well, we're goin', guys. (*There is no comment. Her eyes fasten on* ROCKY – *desperately.*) Say, Rocky, yuh gone deaf? I said me and Chuck was goin' now.

ROCKY (*wiping the bar – with elaborate indifference*). Well, goodbye. Give my love to Joisey.

CORA (*tearfully indignant*). Ain't yuh goin' to wish us happiness, yuh doity little Ginny?

ROCKY. Sure. Here's hopin' yuh don't moider each odder before next week.

CHUCK (*angrily*). Aw, Baby, what d'we care for dat pimp? (ROCKY *turns on him threateningly, but* CHUCK *hears someone upstairs in the hall and grabs* CORA's *arm.*) Here's Hickey comin'! Let's get outa here!

They hurry into the hall. The street door is heard slamming behind them.

ROCKY (*gloomily pronounces an obituary*). One regular guy and one all-right tart gone to hell! (*Fiercely.*) Dat louse Hickey oughta be croaked!

There is a muttered growl of assent from most of the gathering. Then HARRY HOPE *enters from the hall, followed by* JIMMY TOMORROW, *with* HICKEY *on his heels.* HOPE *and* JIMMY *are both putting up a front of self-assurance, but* CORA's *description of them was apt. There is a desperate bluff in their manner as they walk in, which suggests the last march of the condemned.* HOPE *is dressed in an old black Sunday suit, black tie, shoes, socks, which give him the appearance of being in mourning.* JIMMY's *clothes are*

*pressed, his shoes shined, his white linen immaculate. He has a
hangover and his gently appealing dog's eyes have a boiled look.
HICKEY's face is a bit drawn from lack of sleep and his voice is
hoarse from continued talking, but his bustling energy appears
nervously intensified, and his beaming expression is one of triumphant
accomplishment.*

HICKEY. Well, here we are! We've got this far, at least! (*He pats
JIMMY on the back.*) Good work, Jimmy. I told you you weren't
half as sick as you pretended. No excuse whatever for
postponing –

JIMMY. I'll thank you to keep your hands off me! I merely
mentioned I would feel more fit tomorrow. But it might as well
be today, I suppose.

HICKEY. Finish it now, so it'll be dead for ever, and you can be
free! (*He passes him to clap HOPE encouragingly on the shoulder.*)
Cheer up, Harry. You found your rheumatism didn't bother
you coming downstairs, didn't you? I told you it wouldn't. (*He
winks around at the others. With the exception of HUGO and
PARRITT, all their eyes are fixed on him with bitter animosity. He
gives HOPE a playful nudge in the ribs.*) You're the damnedest
one for alibis, Governor! As bad as Jimmy!

HOPE (*putting on his deaf manner*). Eh? I can't hear – (*Defiantly.*)
You're a liar! I've had rheumatism on and off for twenty years.
Ever since Bessie died. Everybody knows that.

HICKEY. Yes, we know it's the kind of rheumatism you turn on
and off! We're on to you, you old faker! (*He claps him on the
shoulder again, chuckling.*)

HOPE (*looks humiliated and guilty – by way of escape he glares around
at the others*). Bejees, what are all you bums hanging round
staring at me for? Think you was watching a circus! Why don't
you get the hell out of here and 'tend to your own business,
like Hickey's told you?

*They look at him reproachfully, their eyes hurt. They fidget as if trying
to move.*

HICKEY. Yes, Harry, I certainly thought they'd have had the
guts to be gone by this time. (*He grins.*) Or maybe I did have
my doubts. (*Abruptly he becomes sincerely sympathetic and earnest.*)
Because I know exactly what you're up against, boys. I know
how damned yellow a man can be when it comes to making
himself face the truth. I've been through the mill, and I had to
face a worse bastard in myself than any of you will have to in

yourselves. I know you become such a coward you'll grab at any lousy excuse to get out of killing your pipe dreams. And yet, as I've told you over and over, it's exactly those damned tomorrow dreams which keep you from making peace with yourself. So you've got to kill them like I did mine. (*He pauses. They glare at him with fear and hatred. They seem about to curse him, to spring at him. But they remain silent and motionless. His manner changes and he becomes kindly bullying.*) Come on boys! Get moving! Who'll start the ball rolling? You, Captain, and you, General. You're nearest the door. And besides, you're old war heroes! You ought to lead the forlorn hope! Come on, now, show us a little of that good old battle of Modder River spirit we've heard so much about! You can't hang around all day looking as if you were scared the street outside would bite you!

LEWIS (*turns with humiliated rage – with an attempt at jaunty casualness*). Right you are, Mister Bloody Nosey Parker! Time I pushed off. Was only waiting to say goodbye to you, Harry, old chum.

HOPE (*dejectedly*). Goodbye, Captain. Hope you have luck.

LEWIS. Oh, I'm bound to, Old Chap, and the same to you.

He pushes the swinging doors open and makes a brave exit, turning to his right and marching off outside the window at right of door.

WETJOEN. Py Gott, if dot Limey can, I can!

He pushes the door open and lumbers through it like a bull charging an obstacle. He turns left and disappears off rear, outside the farthest window.

HICKEY (*exhortingly*). Next? Come on, Ed. It's a fine summer's day and the call of the old circus lot must be in your blood!

MOSHER *glares at him, then goes to the door.* MCGLOIN *jumps up from his chair and starts moving towards the door.* HICKEY *claps him on the back as he passes.*

That's the stuff, Mac.

MOSHER. Goodbye, Harry.

He goes out, turning right outside.

MCGLOIN (*glowering after him*). If that crooked grifter has the guts –

He goes out, turning left outside. HICKEY *glances at* WILLIE *who, before he can speak, jumps from his chair.*

WILLIE. Goodbye, Harry, and thanks for all your kindness.

HICKEY (*claps him on the back*). That's the way, Willie! The DA's a busy man. He can't wait all day for you, you know.

WILLIE *hurries to the door.*

HOPE (*dully*). Good luck, Willie.

WILLIE *goes out and turns right outside. While he is doing so, JIMMY, in a sick panic, sneaks to the bar and furtively reaches for LARRY's glass of whisky.*

HICKEY. And now it's your turn, Jimmy, old pal. (*He sees what JIMMY is at and grabs his arm just as he is about to down the drink.*) Now, now, Jimmy! You can't do that to yourself. One drink on top of your hangover and an empty stomach and you'll be oreyeyed. Then you'll tell yourself you wouldn't stand a chance if you went up soused to get your old job back.

JIMMY (*pleads abjectly*). Tomorrow! I will tomorrow! I'll be in good shape tomorrow! (*Abruptly getting control of himself – with shaken firmness.*) All right. I'm going. Take your hands off me.

HICKEY. That's the ticket! You'll thank me when it's all over.

JIMMY (*in a burst of futile fury*). You dirty swine!

He tries to throw the drink in HICKEY's face, but his aim is poor and it lands on HICKEY's coat. JIMMY turns and dashes through the door, disappearing outside the window at right of door.

HICKEY (*brushing the whisky off his coat – humorously*). All set for an alcohol rub! But no hard feelings. I know how he feels. I wrote the book. I've seen the day when if anyone forced me to face the truth about my pipe dreams, I'd have shot them dead. (*He turns to HOPE – encouragingly.*) Well, Governor, Jimmy made the grade. It's up to you. If he's got the gurs to go through with the test, then certainly you –

LARRY (*bursts out*). Leave Harry alone, damn you!

HICKEY (*grins at him*). I'd make up my mind about myself if I was you, Larry, and not bother over Harry. He'll come through all right. I've promised him that. He doesn't need anyone's bum pity. Do you, Governor?

HOPE (*with a pathetic attempt at his old fuming assertiveness*). No, bejees! Keep your nose out of this, Larry. What's Hickey got to do with it? I've always been going to take this walk, ain't I? Bejees, you bums want to keep me locked up in here 's if I was in jail! I've stood it long enough! I'm free, white and twenty-one, and I'll do as I damned please, bejees! You keep your nose out, too, Hickey! You'd think you was boss of this dump, not me. Sure, I'm all right! Why shouldn't I be? What the hell's to be scared of, just taking a stroll around my own ward? (*As he talks he has been moving towards the door. Now he reaches it.*) What's the weather like outside, Rocky?

ROCKY. Fine day, Boss.

HOPE. What's that? Can't hear you. Don't look fine to me. Looks s if it'd pour down cats and dogs any minute. My rheumatism – (*He catches himself.*) No, must be my eyes. Half blind, bejees. Makes things look black. I see now it's a fine day. Too damned hot for a walk, though, if you ask me. Well, do me good to sweat the booze out of me. But I'll have to watch out for the damned automobiles. Wasn't none of them around the last time, twenty years ago. From what I've seen of 'em through the window, they'd run over you as soon as look at you. Not that I'm scared of 'em. I can take care of myself. (*He puts a reluctant hand on the swinging door.*) Well, so long – (*He stops and looks back – with frightened irascibility.*) Bejees, where are you, Hickey? It's time we got started.

HICKEY (*grins and shakes his head*). No, Harry. Can't be done. You've got to keep a date with yourself alone.

HOPE (*with forced fuming*). Hell of a guy, you are! Thought you'd be willing to help me across the street, knowing I'm half blind. Half deaf, too. Can't hear those damned automobiles. Hell with you! Bejees, I've never needed no one's help and I don't now! (*Egging himself on.*) I'll take a good long walk now I've started. See all my old friends. Bejees, they must have given me up for dead. Twenty years is a long time. But they know it was grief over Bessie's death that made my – (*He puts his hand on the door.*) Well, the sooner I get started – (*Then he drops his hand – with sentimental melancholy.*) You know, Hickey, that's what gets me. Can't help thinking the last time I went out was to Bessie's funeral. After she'd gone, I didn't feel life was worth living. Swore I'd never go out again. (*Pathetically.*) Somehow, I can't feel it's right for me to go, Hickey, even now. It's like I was doing wrong to her memory.

HICKEY. Now Governor, you can't let yourself get away with that one any more!

HOPE (*cupping his hand to his ear*). What's that? Can't hear you. (*Sentimentally again but with desperation.*) I remember now clear as

day the last time before she – It was a fine Sunday morning.
We went out to church together. (*His voice breaks on a sob.*)

HICKEY (*amused*). It's a great act, Governor. But I know better,
and so do you. You never did want to go to church or any
place else with her. She was always on your neck, making you
have ambition and go out and do things, when all yiou wanted
was to get drunk in peace.

HOPE (*falteringly*). Can't hear a word you're saying. You're a
God-damned liar, anyway! (*Then in a sudden fury, his voice
trembling with hatred.*) Bejees, you son of a bitch, if there was a
mad dog outside I'd go and shake hands with it rather than
stay here with you!

*The momentum of his fit of rage does it. He pushes the door open and
strides blindly out into the street and as blindly past the window behind
the free-lunch counter.*

ROCKY (*in amazement*). Jees, he made it! I'd a give yuh fifty to
one he'd never – (*He goes to the end of the bar to look through the
window – disgustedly.*) Aw, he's stopped. I'll bet yuh he comin'
back.

HICKEY. Of course, he's coming back. So are all the others. By
tonight they'll all be here again. You dumbell, that's the whole
point.

ROCKY (*excitedly*). No, he ain't neider! He's gone to de coib. He's
lookin' up and down. Scared stiff of automobiles. Jees, dey ain't
more'n two an hour comes down dis street, de old boob! (*He
watches excitedly, as if it were a race he had a bet on, oblivious to what
happens in the bar.*)

LARRY (*turns on* HICKEY *with bitter defiance*). And now it's my
turn, I suppose? What is it I'm to do to achieve this blessed
peace of yours?

HICKEY (*grins at him*). Why, we've discussed all that, Larry. Just
stop lying to yourself –

LARRY. You think when I say I'm finished with life, and tired of
watching the stupid greed of the human circus, and I'll
welcome closing my eyes in the long sleep of death – you think
that's a coward's lie?

HICKEY (*chuckling*). Well, what do you think, Larry?

LARRY (*with increasing bitter intensity, more as if he were fighting with
himself than with* HICKEY). I'm afraid to live, am I? – and even

more afraid to die! So I sit here, with my pride drowned on the bottom of a bottle, keeping drunk so I won't see myself shaking in my britches with fright, or hear myself whining and praying: Beloved Christ, let me live a little longer at any price! If it's only for a few days more, or a few hours even, have mercy, Almighty God, and let me still clutch greedily to my yellow heart this sweet treasure, this jewel beyond price, the dirty, stinking bit of withered old flesh which is my beautiful little life! (*He laughs with a sneering, vindictive self-loathing, staring inward at himself with contempt and hatred. Then abruptly he makes* HICKEY *again the antagonist.*) You think you'll make me admit that to myself?

HICKEY (*chuckling*). But you just did admit it, didn't you?

PARRITT (*lifts his head from his hands to glare at* LARRY – *jeeringly*). That's the stuff, Hickey! Show the old yellow faker up! He can't play dead on me like this! He's got to help me!

HICKEY. Yes, Larry, you've got to settle with him. I'm leaving you entirely in his hands. He'll do as good a job as I could at making you give up that old grandstand bluff.

LARRY (*angrily*). I'll see the two of you in hell first!

ROCKY (*calls excitedly from the end of the bar*). Jees, Harry's startin' across de street! He's goin' to fool yuh, Hickey, yuh bastard! (*He pauses, watching – then worriedly.*) What de hell's he stoppin' for? Right in de middle of de street! Yuh'd tink he was paralysed or somethin'! (*Disgustedly.*) Aw, he's quittin'! He's turned back! Jees, look at de old bastard travel! Here he comes!

HOPE *passes the window outside the free-lunch counter in a shambling, panic-stricken run. He comes lurching blindly through the swinging doors and stumbles to the bar at* LARRY's *right.*

HOPE. Bejees, give me a drink quick! Scared me out of a year's growth! Bejees, that guy ought to be pinched! Bejees, it ain't safe to walk in the streets! Bejees, that ends me! Never again! Give me that bottle! (*He slops a glass full and drains it and pours another – to* ROCKY, *who is regarding him with scorn – appealingly.*) You seen it, didn't you, Rocky?

ROCKY. Seen what?

HOPE. That automobile, you dumb Wop! Feller driving it must be drunk or crazy. He'd run right over me if I hadn't jumped. (*Ingratiatingly.*) Come on, Larry, have a drink. Everybody have a drink. Have a cigar, Rocky. I know you hardly ever touch it.

ROCKY (*resentfully*). Well, dis is de time I do touch it! (*Pouring a drink.*) I'm goin' to get stinko, see! And if yuh don't like it, yuh know what yuh can do! I gotta good mind to chuck my job, anyway. (*Disgustedly.*) Jees, Harry, I thought yuh had some guts! I was bettin' yuh'd make it and show dat four-flusher up. (*He nods at* HICKEY – *then snorts.*) Automobile, hell! Who d'yuh tink yuh're kiddin'? Dey wasn' no automobile! Yuh just quit cold!

HOPE (*feebly*). Guess I ought to know! Bejees, it almost killed me!

HICKEY (*comes to the bar between him and* LARRY, *and puts a hand on his shoulder – kindly*). Now, now, Governor. Don't be foolish. You've faced the test and come through. You're rid of all that nagging dream stuff now. You know you can't believe it any more.

HOPE (*appeals pleadingly to* LARRY). Larry, you saw it, didn't you? Drink up! Have another! Have all you want! Bejees, we'll go on a grand old souse together! You saw that automobile, didn't you?

LARRY (*compassionately, avoiding his eyes*). Sure, I saw it, Harry. You had a narrow escape. Be God, I thought you were a goner!

HICKEY (*turns on him with a flash of sincere indignation*). What the hell's the matter with you, Larry? You know what I told you about the wrong kind of pity. Leave Harry alone! You'd think I was trying to harm him, the fool way you act! My oldest friend! What kind of a louse do you think I am? There isn't anything I wouldn't do for Harry, and he knows it! All I've wanted to do is fix it so he'll be finally at peace with himself for the rest of his days! And if you'll only wait until the final returns are in, you'll find that's exactly what I've accomplished! (*He turns to* HOPE *and pats his shoulder – coaxingly.*) Come now, Governor. What's the use of being stubborn, now when it's all over and dead? Give up that ghost automobile.

HOPE (*beginning to collapse within himself – dully*). Yes, what's the use – now? All a lie! No automobile. But, bejees, something ran over me! Must have been myself, I guess. (*He forces a feeble smile – then wearily,*) Guess I'll sit down. Feel all in. Like a corpse, bejees. (*He picks a bottle and glass from the bar and walks to the first table and slumps down in the chair, facing left-front. His shaking hand misjudges the distance and he sets the bottle on the table with a jar that rouses* HUGO, *who lifts his head from his arms and blinks at him through his thick spectacles.* HOPE *speaks to him in a flat, dead voice.*) Hello, Hugo. Coming up for air? Stay passed out, that's the right dope. There ain't any cool willow trees – except you grow your own in a bottle. (*He pours a drink and gulps it down.*)

HUGO (*with his silly giggle*). Hello, Harry, stupid proletarian monkey-face! I vill trink champagne beneath the villow – (*With a change to aristocratic fastidiousness.*) But the slaves must ice it properly! (*With guttural rage.*) Gottamned Hickey! Peddler pimp for nouveau-riche capitalism! Vhen I lead the jackass mob to the sack of Babylon, I vill make them hang him to a lamp-post the first one!

HOPE (*spiritlessly*). Good work. I'll help pull up the rope. Have a drink, Hugo.

HUGO (*frightenedly*). No, thank you. I am too trunk now. I hear myself say crazy things. Do not listen, please. Larry vill tell you I haf never been so crazy trunk. I must sleep it off. (*He starts to put his head on his arms but stops and stares at* HOPE *with growing uneasiness.*) Vhat's matter, Harry? You look funny. You look dead. Vhat's happened? I don't know you. Listen, I feel I am dying, too. Because I am so crazy trunk! It is very necessary I sleep. But I can't sleep here vith you. You look dead. (*He scrambles to his feet in a confused panic, turns his back on* HOPE *and settles into the chair at the next table which faces left. He thrusts his head down on his arms like an ostrich hiding its head in the sand. He does not notice* PARRITT, *nor* PARRITT *him.*)

LARRY (*to* HICKEY *with bitter condemnation*). Another one who's begun to enjoy your peace!

HICKEY. Oh, I know it's tough on him right now, the same as it is on Harry. But that's only the first shock. I promise you they'll both come through all right.

LARRY. And you believe that! I see you do! You mad fool!

HICKEY. Of course, I believe it! I tell you I know from my own experience!

HOPE (*spiritlessly*). Close that big clam of yours, Hickey. Bejees, you're a worse gabber than that nagging bitch, Bessie, was. (*He drinks his drink mechanically and pours another.*)

ROCKY (*in amazement*). Jees, did yuh hear dat?

HOPE (*dully*). What's wrong with this booze? There's no kick in it.

ROCKY (*worriedly*). Jees, Larry, Hugo had it right. He does look like he'd croaked.

HICKEY (*annoyed*). Don't be a damned fool! Give him time. He's coming along all right. (*He calls to* HOPE *with a first trace of underlying uneasiness.*) You're all right, aren't you, Harry?

HOPE (*dully*). I want to pass out like Hugo.

LARRY (*turns to* HICKEY – *with bitter anger*). It's the peace of death you've brought him.

HICKEY (*for the first time loses his temper*). That's a lie! (*But he controls this instantly and grins.*) Well, well, you did manage to get a rise out of me that time. I think such a hell of a lot of Harry – (*Impatiently,*) You know that's damned foolishness. Look at me. I've been through it. Do I look dead? Just leave Harry alone and wait until the shock wears off and you'll see. He'll be a new man. Like I am. (*He calls to* HOPE *coaxingly.*) How's it coming, Governor? Beginning to feel free, aren't you? Relieved and not guilty any more?

HOPE (*grumbles spiritlessly*). Bejees, you must have been monkeying with the booze, too, you interfering bastard! There's no life in it now. I want to get drunk and pass out. Let's all pass out. Who the hell cares?

HICKEY (*lowering his voice – worriedly to* LARRY). I admit I didn't think he'd be hit so hard. He's always been a happy-go-lucky slob. Like I was. Of course, it hit me hard, too. But only for a minute. Then I felt as if a ton of guilt had been lifted off my mind. I saw what had happened was the only possible way for the peace of all concerned.

LARRY (*sharply*). What was it happened? Tell us that! And don't try to get out of it! I want a straight answer! (*Vindictively.*) I think it was something you drove someone else to do!

HICKEY (*puzzled*). Someone else?

LARRY (*accusingly*). What did your wife die of? You've kept that a deep secret, I notice – for some reason!

HICKEY (*reproachfully*). You're not very considerate, Larry. But, if you insist on knowing now, there's no reason you shouldn't. It was a bullet through the head that killed Evelyn.

There is a second's tense silence.

HOPE (*dully*). Who the hell cares? To hell with her and that nagging old hag, Bessie.

ROCKY. Christ. You had de right dope, Larry.

LARRY (*revengefully*). You drove your poor wife to suicide? I
knew it! Be God, I don't blame her! I'd almost do as much
myself to be rid of you! It's what you'd like to drive us all to –
(*Abruptly he is ashamed of himself and pitying.*) I'm sorry, Hickey.
I'm a rotten louse to throw that in your face.

HICKEY (*quietly*). Oh, that's all right, Larry. But don't jump at
conclusions. I didn't say poor Evelyn committed suicide. It's the
last thing she'd ever have done, as long as I was alive for her to
take care of and forgive. If you'd known her at all, you'd never
get such a crazy suspicion. (*He pauses – then slowly.*) No, I'm
sorry to have to tell you my poor wife was killed.

LARRY *stares at him with growing horror and shrinks back along the
bar away from him.* PARRITT *jerks his head up from his hands and
looks around frightenedly, not at* HICKEY, *but at* LARRY.
ROCKY's *round eyes are popping.* HOPE *stares dully at the table top.*
HUGO, *his head hidden in his arms, gives no sign of life.*

LARRY (*shakenly*). Then she – was murdered.

PARRITT (*springs to his feet – stammers defensively*). You're a liar,
Larry! You must be crazy to say that to me! You know she's still
alive!

But no one pays any attention to him.

ROCKY (*blurts out*). Moidered? Who done it?

LARRY (*his eyes fixed with fascinated horror on* HICKEY –
frightenedly). Don't ask questions, you dumb Wop! It's none of
our damned business! Leave Hickey alone!

HICKEY (*smiles at him with affectionate amuzement*). Still the old
grandstand bluff, Larry? Or is it some more bum pity? (*He
turns to* ROCKY – *matter-of-factly.*) The police don't know who
killed her yet, Rocky. But I expect they will before very long.
(*As if that finished the subject, he comes forward to* HOPE *and sits
beside him, with an arm around his shoulder – affectionately coaxing.*)
Coming along fine now, aren't you, Governor? Getting over the
first shock? Beginning to feel free from guilt and lying hopes
and at peace with yourself?

HOPE (*with a dull callousness*). Somebody croaked your Evelyn,
eh? Bejees, my bets are on the iceman! But who the hell cares?
Let's get drunk and pass out. (*He tosses down his drink with a
lifeless, automatic movement – complainingly.*) Bejees, what did you
do to the booze, Hickey? There's no damned life left in it.

PARRITT (*stammers, his eyes on* LARRY, *whose eyes in turn remain fixed on* HICKEY). Don't look like that, Larry! You've got to believe what I told you! It had nothing to do with her! It was just to get a few lousy dollars!

HUGO (*suddenly raises his head from his arms and, looking straight in front of him, pounds on the table frightenedly with his small fists*). Don't be a fool! Buy me a trink! But no more vine! It is not properly iced!! (*With guttural rage.*) Gottamned stupid proletarian slaves! Buy me a trink or I vill have you shot! (*He collapses into abject begging.*) Please, for Gott's sake! I am not trunk enough! I cannot sleep! Life is a crazy monkey-face! Always there is blood beneath the villow trees! I hate it and I am afraid! (*He hides his face on his arms, sobbing muffledly.*) Please, I am crazy trunk! I say crazy things! For Gott's sake, do not listen to me!

But no one pays any attention to him. LARRY *stands shrunk back against the bar.* ROCKY *is leaning over it. They stare at* HICKEY. PARRITT *stands looking pleadingly at* LARRY.

HICKEY (*gazes with worried kindliness at* HOPE). You're beginning to worry me, Governor. Something's holding you up somewhere. I don't see why – You've faced the truth about yourself. You've done what you had to do to kill your nagging pipe dreams. Oh, I know it knocks you cold. But only for a minute. then you see it was the only possible way to peace. And you feel happy. Like I did. That's what worries me about you, Governor. It's time you began to feel happy –

Curtain.

ACT FOUR

Scene. Same as Act One – the back room with the curtain separating it from the section of the bar-room with its single table at right of curtain, front. It is around half-past one in the morning of the following day.

The tables in the back room have a new arrangement. The one at left, front, before the window to the yard, is in the same position. So is the one at the right, rear, of it in the second row. But this table now has only one chair. This chair is at right of it, facing directly front. The two tables on either side of the door at rear are unchanged. But the table which was at centre, front, has been pushed towards right so that it and the table at right, rear, of it in the second row, and the last table at right in the front row, are now jammed so closely together that they form one group.

LARRY, HUGO *and* PARRITT *are at the table at left, front.* LARRY *is at left of it, beside the window, facing front.* HUGO *sits at rear, facing front, his head on his arms in his habitual position, but he is not asleep. On* HUGO's *left is* PARRITT, *his chair facing left, front. At right of table, an empty chair, facing left.* LARRY's *chin is on his chest, his eyes fixed on the floor. He will not look at* PARRITT, *who keeps staring at him with a sneering, pleading challenge.*

Two bottles of whisky are on each table, whisky and chaser glasses, a pitcher of water.

The one chair by the table at right, rear, of them is vacant.

At the first table at right of centre, CORA *sits at left, front, of it, facing front. Around the rear of this table are four empty chairs. Opposite* CORA, *in a sixth chair, is* CAPTAIN LEWIS, *also facing front. On his left,* MCGLOIN *is facing front in a chair before the middle table of his group. At right, rear, of him, also at this table,* GENERAL WETJOEN *sits facing front. In back of this table are three empty chairs.*

At right, rear, of WETJOEN, *but beside the last table of the group, sits* WILLIE. *On* WILLIE's *left, at rear of table, is* HOPE. *On* HOPE's *left, at right, rear of table, is* MOSHER. *Finally, at right of table is* JIMMY TOMORROW. *All of the four sit facing front.*

There is an atmosphere of oppressive stagnation in the room, and a quality of insensibility about all the people in this group at right. They are like wax figures, set stiffly on their chairs, carrying out mechanically the

*motions of getting drunk but sunk in a numb stupor which is impervious
to stimulation.*

*In the bar section, JOE is sprawled in the chair at right of table, facing
left. His head rolls forward in a sodden slumber. ROCKY is standing
behind his chair, regarding him with dull hostility. ROCKY's face is set
in an expression of tired, callous toughness. He looks now like a minor
Wop gangster.*

ROCKY (*shakes* JOE *by the shoulder*). Come on, yuh damned
nigger! Beat it in de back room! It's after hours. (*But* JOE
remains inert. ROCKY *gives up.*) Aw, to hell wid it. Let de dump
get pinched. I'm through wid dis lousy job, anyway! (*He hears
someone at rear and calls.*) Who's dat?

CHUCK *appears from rear. He has been drinking heavily, but there is
no lift to his jag; his manner is grouchy and sullen. He has evidently
been brawling. His knuckles are raw and there is a mouse under one
eye. He has lost his straw hat, his tie is awry, and his blue suit is dirty.*
ROCKY *eyes him indifferently.*

Been scrappin', huh? Started off on your periodical, ain't yuh?
(*For a second there is a gleam of satisfaction in his eyes.*)

CHUCK. Yeah, ain't yuh glad? (*Truculently.*) What's it to yuh?

ROCKY. Not a damn ting. But dis is someting to me. I'm out on
my feet holdin' down your job. Yuh said if I'd take your day,
yuh'd relieve me at six, and here it's half-past one a.m. Well,
yuh're takin' over now, get me, no matter how plastered yuh
are!

CHUCK. Plastered, hell! I wisht I was. I've lapped up a gallon,
but it don't hit me right. And to hell wid de job. I'm goin' to
tell Harry I'm quittin'.

ROCKY. Yeah? Well, I'm quittin', too.

CHUCK. I've played sucker for dat crummy blonde long enough,
lettin' her kid me into woikin'. From now on I take it easy.

ROCKY. I'm glad yuh're gettin' some sense.

CHUCK. And I hope yuh're gettin' some. What a prize sap you
been, tendin' bar when yuh got two good hustlers in your
stable!

ROCKY. Yeah, but I ain't no sap now. I'll loin dem, when dey
get back fron Coney. (*Sneering.*) Jees, dat Cora sure played you
for a dope, feedin' yuh dat marriage-on-de-farm hop!

CHUCK (*dully*). Yeah. Hickey got it right. A lousy pipe dream. It was her pulling sherry flips on me woke me up. All de way walkin' to de ferry, every ginmill we come to she'd drag me in to blow her. I got tinkin', Christ, what won't she want when she gets de ring on her finger and I'm hooked? So I tells her at de ferry, 'Kiddo, yuh can go to Joisey, or to hell, but count me out.'

ROCKY. She says it was her told you to go to hell, because yuh'd started hittin' de booze.

CHUCK (*ignoring this*). I got tinkin', too Jees, won't I look sweet wid a wife dat if yuh put all de guys she's stayed wid side by side, dey's reach to Chicago. (*He sighs gloomily.*) Dat kind of dame, yuh can't rrust 'em. De minute your back is toined, dey're cheatin' wid de iceman or someone. Hickey done me a favour, makin' me wake up. (*He pauses – then adds pathetically.*) On'y it was fun, kinda, me and Cora kiddin' ourselves – (*Suddenly his face hardens with hatred.*) Where is dat son of a bitch, Hickey? I want one good sock at dat guy – just one! – and de next buttin' in he'll do will be in de morgue! I'll take a chance on goin' to the Chair – !

ROCKY (*starts – in a low warning voice*). Piano! Keep away from him, Chuck! He ain't here now, anyway. He went out to phone, he said. He wouldn't call from here. I got a hunch he's beat it. But if he does come back yuh don't know him, if anyone asks yuh, get me? (*As CHUCK looks at him with dull surprise he lowers his voice to a whisper.*) De Chair, maybe dat's where he's goin'. I don't know nuttin', see, but it looks like he croaked his wife.

CHUCK (*with a flash of interest*). Yuh mean she really was cheatin' on him? Den I don't blame de guy –

ROCKY. Who's blamin' him? When a dame asks for it – But I don't know nuttin' about it, see?

CHUCK. Is any of de gang wise?

ROCKY. Larry is. And de boss ought to be. I tried to wise de rest of dem up to stay clear of him, but dey're all so licked, I don't know if dey got it. (*He pauses – vindictively.*) I don't give a damn what he done to his wife, but if he gets de Hot Seat I won't go into no mournin'!

CHUCK. Me, neider!

ROCKY. Not after his trowin' it in my face I'm a pimp. What if I am? Why de hell not? And what he's done to Harry. Jees, de poor old slob is so licked he can't even get drunk. And all de gang. Dey're all licked. I couldn't help feelin' sorry for de poor bums when dey showed up tonight, one by one, lookin' like pooches wid deir tails between deir legs, dat everyone'd been kickin' till dey was too punch-drunk to feel it no more. Jimmy Tomorrow was de last. Schwartz, de copper, brung him in. Seen him sittin' on de dock on West Street, lookin' at de water and cryin'! Schwartz thought he was drunk and I let him tink it. But he was cold sober. He was tryin' to jump in and didn't have de noive, I figgered it. Noive! Jess, dere ain't enough guts left in de whole gang to battle a mosquito!

CHUCK. Aw, to tell wid 'em! Who cares? Gimme a drink.

ROCKY *pushes the bottle toward him apathetically.*

I see you been hittin' de redeye, too.

ROCKY. Yeah. But it don't do no good. I can't get drunk right.

CHUCK *drinks.* JOE *mumbles in his sleep.* CHUCK *regards him resentfully.*

Dis doity dinge was able to get his snootful and pass out. Jees, even Hickey can't faze a nigger! Yuh'd tink he was fazed if yuh'd seen him come in. Stinko, and he pulled a gat and said he'd plug Hickey for insultin' him. Den he dropped it and begun to cry and said he wasn't a gamblin' man or a tough guy no more; he was yellow. He'd borrowed de gat to stick up someone, and den didn't have de guts. He got drunk panhandlin' drinks in nigger joints, I s'pose. I guess dey felt sorry for him.

CHUCK. He ain't got no business in de bar after hours. Why don't yuh chuck him out?

ROCKY (*apathetically*). Aw, to hell wid it. Who cares?

CHUCK (*lapsing into the same mood*). Yeah. I don't.

JOE (*suddenly lunges to his feet dazedly – mumbles in humbled apology*). Scuse me, White Boys. Scuse me for livin'. I don't want to be where I's not wanted. (*He makes his way swayingly to the opening in the curtain at rear and tacks down to the middle table of the three at right, front. He feels his way around it to the table at its left and gets to the chair in back of* CAPTAIN LEWIS.)

CHUCK (*gets up – in a callous, brutal tone*). My pig's in de back room, ain't she? I wanna collect de dough I wouldn't take dis mornin', like a sucker, before she blows it. (*He goes rear.*)

ROCKY (*getting up*). I'm comin', too. I'm trough woikin'. I ain't no lousy bartender.

CHUCK *comes through the curtain and looks for* CORA *as* JOE *flops down in the chair in back of* CAPTAIN LEWIS.

JOE (*taps* LEWIS *on the shoulder – servilely apologetic*). If you objects to my sittin' here, Captain, just tell me and I pulls my freight.

LEWIS. No apology required, old chap. Anybody could tell you I should feel honoured a bloody Kaffir would lower himself to sit beside me.

JOE *stares at him with sodden perplexity – then closes his eyes.* CHUCK *comes forward to take the chair behind* CORA's, *as* ROCKY *enters the back room and starts over toward* LARRY's *table.*

CHUCK (*his voice hard*). I'm waitin', Baby. Dig!

CORA (*with apathetic obedience*). Sure. I been expectin' yuh. I got it all ready. Here.

She passes a small roll of bills she has in her hand over her shoulder, without looking at him. He takes it, glances at it suspiciously, then shoves it in his pocket without a word of acknowledgment. CORA *speaks with a tired wonder at herself rather than resentment toward him.*

Jees, imagine me kiddin' myself I wanted to marry a drunken pimp.

CHUCK. Dat's nuttin', Baby. Imagine de sap I'da been, when I can get your dough just as easy widout it!

ROCKY (*takes the chair on* PARRITT's *left, facing* LARRY – *dully*). Hello, Old Cemetery. (LARRY *doesn't seem to hear. To* PARRITT.) Hello, Tightwad. You still around?

PARRITT (*keeps his eyes on* LARRY – *in a jeeringly challenging tone*). Ask Larry! he knows I'm here, all right, although he's pretending not to! He'd like to forget I'm alive! He's trying to kid himself with that grandstand philosopher stuff! But he knows he can't get away with it now! He kept himself locked in his room until a while ago, alone with a bottle of booze, but he couldn't make it work! He couldn't even get drunk! He had to come out! There must have been something there he was even more scared to face than he is Hickey and me! I guess he got looking at the fire escape and thinking how handy it was, if he was really sick of life and only had the nerve to die! (*He pauses sneeringly.*)

LARRY's *face has tautened, but he pretends he doesn't hear.* ROCKY *pays no attention. His head has sunk forward, and he stares at the table top, sunk in the same stupor as the other occupants of the room.* PARRITT *goes on, his tone becoming more insistent.*

He's been thinking of me, too, Rocky. Trying to figure a way to get out of helping me! He doesn't want to be bothered understanding. But he does understand all right! He used to love her, too. So he thinks I ought to take a hop off the fire escape! (*He pauses.*)

LARRY's *hands on the table have clinched into fists, as his nails dig into his palms, but he remains silent.* PARRITT *breaks and starts pleading.*

For God's sake, Larry, can't you say something? Hickey's got me all balled up. Thinking of what he must have done has got me so I don't know any more what I did or why. I can't go on like this! I've got to know what I ought to do –

LARRY (*in a stifled tone*). God damn you? Are you trying to make me your executioner?

PARRITT (*starts frightenedly*). Execution? Then you do think – ?

LARRY. I don't think anything!

PARRITT (*with forced jeering*). I suppose you think I ought to die because I sold out a lot of loud-mouthed fakers, who were cheating suckers with a phony pipe dream, and put them where they ought to be, in jail? (*He forces a laugh.*) Don't make me laugh! I ought to get a medal! What a damned old sap you are! You must still believe in the Movement! (*He nudges* ROCKY *with his elbow.*) Hickey's right about him, isn't he, Rocky? An old no-good drunken tramp, as dumb as he is, ought to take a hop off the fire escape!

ROCKY (*dully*). Sure. Why don't he? Or you? Or me? What de hell's de difference? Who cares?

There is a faint stir from all the crowd, as if this sentiment struck a responsive chord in their numbed minds. They mumble almost in chorus as one voice, like sleepers talking out of a dully irritating dream, 'The hell with it!' 'Who cares?' *Then the sodden silence descends again on the room.* ROCKY *looks from* PARRITT *to* LARRY *puzzledly. He mutters.*

What am I doin' here wid youse two? I remember I had something on my mind to tell yuh. What – ? Oh, I got it now.

(*He looks from one to the other of their oblivious faces with a strange, sly, calculating look – ingratiatingly.*) I was tinking how you was bot' reg'lar guys. I tinks, ain't two guys like dem saps to be hangin' round like a coupla stew bums and wastin' demselves. Not dat I blame yuh for not woikin'. On'y suckers woik. But dere's no percentage in bein' broke when yuh can grab good jack for yourself and make someone else woik for yuh, is dere? I mean, like I do. So I tinks, Dey're my pals and I ought to wise up two good guys like dem to play my system, and not be lousy barflies, no good to demselves or nobody else. (*He addresses PARRITT now – persuasively.*) What yuh tink, Parritt? Ain't I right? Sure, I am. So don't be a sucker, see? Yuh ain't a bad-lookin' guy. Yuh could easy make some gal who's a good hustler, an' start a stable. I'd help yuh and wise yuh up to de inside dope on de game. (*He pauses inquiringly. PARRITT gives no sign of having heard him. ROCKY asks impatiently.*) Well, what about it? What if dey do call yuh a pimp? What de hell do you care – any more'n I do.

PARRITT (*without looking at him – vindictively*). I'm through with whores. I wish they were all in jail – or dead!

ROCKY (*ignores this – disappointedly*). So yuh won't touch it, huh? Aw right, stay a bum! (*He turns to LARRY.*) Jees, Larry, he's sure one dumb boob, ain't he? Dead from de neck up! He don't know a good ting when he sees it. (*Oily, even persuasive again.*) But how about you, Larry? You ain't dumb. So why not, huh? Sure, yuh're old, but dat don't matter. All de hustlers tink yuh're aces. Dey fall for yuh like yuh was deir uncle or old man or something. Dey'd like takin' care of yuh. And de cops 'round here, dey like yuh, too. It'd be a pipe for yuh, 'specially wid me to help yuh and wise yuh up. Yuh wouldn't have to worry where de next drink's comin' from, or wear doity clothes. (*Hopefully.*) Well, don't it look good to yuh?

LARRY (*glances at him – for a moment he is stirred to sardonic pity*). No, it doesn't look good, Rocky. I mean the peace Hickey's brought you. It isn't contented enough, if you have to make everyone else a pimp, too.

ROCKY (*stares at him stupidly – then pushes his chair back and gets up, grumbling*). I'm a sap to waste time on yuh. A stew bum is a stew bum and yuh can't change him. (*He turns away – then turns back for an afterthought.*) Like I was sayin' to Chuck, yuh better keep away from Hickey. If anyone asks yuh, yuh don't know nuttin', get me? Yuh never even hoid he had a wife. (*His face hardens.*) Jees, we all ought to git drunk and stage a celebration when dat bastard goes to de Chair.

LARRY (*vindictively*). Be God, I'll celebrate with you and drink long life to him in hell! (*Then guiltily and pityingly.*) No! The poor mad devil – (*Then with angry self-contempt.*) Ah, pity again! The wrong kind! He'll welcome the Chair!

PARRITT (*contemptuously*). Yes, what are you so damned scared of death for? I don't want your lousy pity.

ROCKY. Christ, I hope he don't come back, Larry. We don't know nuttin' now. We're on'y guessin', see? But if de bastard keeps on talkin' –

LARRY (*grimly*). He'll come back. He'll keep on talking. He's got to. He's lost his confidence that the peace he's sold us is the real McCoy, and it's made him uneasy about his own. He'll have to prove to us –

As he is speaking HICKEY *appears silently in the doorway at rear. He has lost his beaming salesman's grin. His manner is no longer self-assured. His expression is uneasy, baffled and resentful. It has the stubborn set of an obsessed determination. His eyes are on* LARRY *as he comes in. As he speaks, there is a start from all the crowd, a shrinking away from him.*

HICKEY (*angrily*). That's a damned lie, Larry! I haven't lost confidence a damned bit! Why should I? (*Boastfully.*) By God, whenever I made up my mind to sell someone something I knew they ought to want, I've sold 'em! (*He suddenly looks confused – haltingly.*) I mean – it isn't kind of you, Larry, to make that kind of crack when I've been doing my best to help –

ROCKY (*moving away from him toward right – sharply*). Keep away from me! I don't know nuttin' bout yuh, see? (*His tone is threatening but his manner as he turns his back and ducks quickly across to the bar entrance is that of one in flight. In the bar he comes forward and slumps in a chair at the table, facing front.*)

HICKEY (*comes to the table at right, rear, of* LARRY's *table and sits in the one chair there, facing front. He looks over the crowd at right, hopefully and then disappointedly. He speaks with a strained attempt at his old affectionate jollying manner*). Well, well! How are you coming along, everybody? Sorry I had to leave you for a while, but there was something I had to get finally settled. It's all fixed now.

HOPE (*in the voice of one reiterating mechanically a hopeless complaint*). When are you going to do something about this booze, Hickey? Bejees, we all know you did something to take the life out of it. It's like drinking dishwater! We can't pass out! And you promised us peace.

His group all join in in a dull, complaining chorus, 'We can't pass out! You promised us peace!'

HICKEY (*bursts into resentful exasperation*). For God's sake, Harry, are you still harping on that damned nonsense! You've kept it up all afternoon and night! And you've got everybody else singing the same crazy tune! I've had about all I can stand – that's why I phoned – (*He controls himself.*) Excuse me, boys and girls. I don't mean that. I'm just worried about you, when you play dead on me like this. I was hoping by the time I got back you'd be like you ought to be! I thought you were deliberately holding back, while I was around, because you didn't want to give me the satisfaction of showing me I'd had the right dope. And I did have! I know from my own experience.
(*Exasperatedly.*) But I've explained that a million times! And you've all done what you needed to do! By rights you should be contented now, without a single damned hope or lying dream left to torment you! But here you are, acting like a lot of stiffs cheating the undertaker! (*He looks around accusingly.*) I can't figure it – unless it's just your damned pigheaded stubbornness! (*He breaks – miserably.*) Hell, you oughtn't to act this way with me! You're my old pals, the only friends I've got. You know the one thing I want is to see you all happy before I go – (*Rousing himself to his old brisk, master-of-ceremonies manner.*) And there's damned little time left now. I've made a date for two o'clock. We've got to get busy right away and find out what's wrong. (*There is a sodden silence. He goes on exasperatedly.*) Can't you appreciate what you've got, for God's sake? Don't you know you're free now to be yourselves, without having to feel remorse or guilt, or lie to yourselves about reforming tomorrow? Can't you see there is no tomorrow now? You're rid of it for ever! You've killed it! You don't have to care a damn about anything any more! You've finally got the game of life licked, don't you see that? (*Angrily exhorting.*) Then why the hell don't you get pie-eyed and celebrate? Why don't you laugh and sing 'Sweet Adeline'? (*With bitterly hurt accusation.*) The only reason I can think of is, you're putting on this rotten half-dead act just to get back at me! Because you hate my guts! (*He breaks again.*) God, don't do that, gang! It makes me feel like hell to think you hate me. It makes me feel you suspect I must have

hated you. But that's a lie! Oh, I know I used to hate everyone
in the world who wasn't as rotten a bastard as I was! But that
was when I was still living in hell – before I faced the truth and
saw the one possible way to free poor Evelyn and give her the
peace she'd always dreamed about. (*He pauses.*)

*Everyone in the group stirs with awakening dread and they all begin to
grow tense on their chairs.*

CHUCK (*without looking at* HICKEY – *with dull, resentful
viciousness*). Aw, put a bag over it! To hell wid Evelyn! What if
she was cheatin'? And who cares what yuh did to her? Dat's
your funeral. We don't give a damn, see?

There is a dull, resentful chorus of assent, 'We don't give a damn,'
CHUCK *adds dully.*

All we want outa you is keep de hell away from us and give us
a rest.

A muttered chorus of assent.

HICKEY (*as if he hadn't heard this – an obsessed look on his face*).
The one possible way to make up to her for all I'd made her go
through, and get her rid of me so I couldn't make her suffer
any more, and she wouldn't have to forgive me again! I saw I
couldn't do it by killing myself, like I wanted to for a long time.
That would have been the last straw for her. She'd have died of
a broken heart to think I could do that to her. She'd have
blamed herself for it, too. Or I couldn't just run away from
her. She'd have died of grief and humiliation if I'd done that to
her. She'd have thought I'd stopped loving her. (*He adds with a
strange impressive simplicity.*) You see, Evelyn loved me. And I
loved her. That was the trouble. It would have been easy to
find a way out if she hadn't loved me so much. Or if I hadn't
loved her. But as it was, there was only one possible way. (*He
pauses – then adds simply.*) I had to kill her.

*There is a second's dead silence as he finishes – then a tense indrawn
breath like a gasp from the crowd, and a general shrinking movement.*

LARRY (*bursts out*). You mad fool, can't you keep your mouth
shut! We may hate you for what you've done this time, but we
remember the old times, too, when you brought kindness and
laughter with you instead of death! We don't want to know
things that will make us help send you to the Chair!

PARRITT (*with angry scorn*). Ah, shut up, you yellow faker! Can't
you face anything? Wouldn't I deserve the Chair, too, if I'd –

It's worse if you kill someone and they have to go on living. I'd be glad of the Chair! It'd wipe it out! It'd square me with myself!

HICKEY (*disturbed – with a movement of repulsion*). I wish you'd get rid of that bastard, Larry. I can't have him pretending there's something in common between him and me. It's what's in your heart that counts. There was love in my heart, not hate.

PARRITT (*glares at him in angry terror*). You're a liar! I don't hate her! I couldn't! And it had nothing to do with her, anyway! You ask Larry!

LARRY (*grabs his shoulder and shakes him furiously*). God damn you, stop shoving your rotten soul in my lap!

PARRITT *subsides, hiding his face in his hands and shuddering.*

HICKEY (*goes on quietly now*). Don't worry about the Chair, Larry. I know it's still hard for you not to be terrified by death, but when you've made peace with yourself, like I have, you won't give a damn. (*He addresses the group at right again – earnestly.*) Listen, everybody. I've made up my mind the only way I can clear things up for you, so you'll realize how contented and carefree you ought to feel, now I've made you get rid of your pipe dreams, is to show you what a pipe dream did to me and Evelyn. I'm certain if I tell you about it from the beginning, you'll appreciate what I've done for you and why I did it, and how damned grateful you ought to be – instead of hating me. (*He begins eagerly in a strange running narrative manner.*) You see, even when we were kids, Evelyn and me –

HOPE (*bursts out, pounding with his glass on the table*). No! Who the hell cares? We don't want to hear it. All we want is to pass out and get drunk and a little peace!

They are all, except LARRY *and* PARRITT, *seized by the same fit and pound with their glasses, even* HUGO, *and* ROCKY *in the bar, and shout in chorus,* 'Who the hell cares? We want to pass out!'

HICKEY (*with an expression of wounded hurt*). All right, if that's the way you feel. I don't want to cram it down your throats. I don't need to tell anyone. I don't feel guilty. I'm only worried about you.

HOPE. What did you do to this booze? That's what we'd like to hear. Bejees, you done something. There's no life or kick in it now. (*He appeals mechanically to* JIMMY TOMORROW.) Ain't that right, Jimmy?

JIMMY (*more than any of them, his face has a wax-figure blankness that makes it look embalmed. He answers in a precise, completely lifeless voice, but his reply is not to* HARRY's *question, and he does not look at him or anyone else*). Yes. Quite right. It was all a stupid lie – my nonsense about tomorrow. Naturally, they would never give me my position back. I would never dream of asking them. It would be hopeless. I didn't resign. I was fired for drunkenness. And that was years ago. I'm much worse now. And it was absurd of me to excuse my drunkenness by pretending it was my wife's adultery that ruined my life. As Hickey guessed, I was a drunkard before that. Long before. I discovered early in life that living frightened me when I was sober. I have forgotten why I married Marjorie. I can't even remember now if she was pretty. She was a blonde, I think, but I couldn't swear to it. I had some idea of wanting a home, perhaps. But, of course, I much preferred the nearest pub. Why Marjorie married me, God knows. It's impossible to believe she loved me. She soon found I much preferred drinking all night with my pals to being in bed with her. So, naturally, she was unfaithful. I didn't blame her. I really didn't care. I was glad to be free – even grateful to her, I think, for giving me such a good tragic excuse to drink as much as I damned well pleased. (*He stops like a mechanical doll that has run down.*)

No one gives any sign of having heard him. There is a heavy silence. Then ROCKY, *at the table in the bar, turns grouchily as he hears a noise behind him. Two men come quietly forward. One,* MORAN, *is middle-aged. The other,* LIEB, *is in his twenties. They look ordinary in every way, without anything distinctive to indicate what they do for a living.*

ROCKY (*grumpily*). In de back room if yuh wanta drink.

MORAN *makes a peremptory sign to be quiet. All of a sudden* ROCKY *senses they are detectives and springs up to face them, his expression freezing into a wary blankness.* MORAN *pulls back his coat to show his badge.*

MORAN (*in a low voice*). Guy named Hickman in the back room?

ROCKY. Tink I know de names of all de guys – ?

MORAN. Listen you! This is murder. And don't be a sap. It was Hickman himself phoned in and said we'd find him here around two.

ROCKY (*dully*). So dat's who he phoned to. (*He shrugs his shoulders.*) Aw right, if he asked for it. He's de fat guy sittin' alone. (*He slumps down in his chair again.*) And if yuh want a confession all yuh got to do is listen. He'll be tellin' all about it soon. Yuh can't stop de bastard talkin'.

MORAN gives him a curious look, then whispers to LIEB, who disappears rear and a moment later appears in the hall doorway of the back room. He spots HICKEY and slides into a chair at the left of the doorway, cutting off escape by the hall. MORAN goes back and stands in the opening in the curtain leading to the back room. He sees HICKEY and stands watching him and listening.

HICKEY (*suddenly bursts out*). I've got to tell you! Your being the way you are now gets my goat! It's all wrong! It puts things in my mind – about myself. It makes me think, if I got balled up about you, how do I know I wasn't balled up about myself? And that's plain damned foolishness. When you know the story of me and Evelyn, you'll see there wasn't any other possible way otu of it, for her sake. Only I've got to start way back at the beginning or you won't understand. (*He starts his story, his tone again becoming musingly reminiscent.*) You see, even as a kid I was always restless. I had to keep on the go. You've heard the old saying, 'Ministers' sons are sons of guns.' Well, that was me, and then some. Home was like a jail. I didn't fall for the religious bunk. Listening to my old man whooping up hell fire and scaring those Hoosier suckers into shelling out their dough only handed me a laugh, although I had to hand it to him, the way he sold them nothing for something. I guess I take after him, and that's what made me a good salesman. Well, anyway, as I said, home was like jail, and so was school, and so was that damned hick town. The only place I liked was the pool rooms, where I could smoke Sweet Caporals, and mop up a couple of beers, thinking I was a hell-on-wheels sport. We had one hooker shop in town, and, of course, I liked that, too. Not that I hardly ever had entrance money. My old man was a tight old bastard. But I liked to sit around in the parlour and joke with the girls, and they liked me because I could kid 'em along and make 'em laugh. Well, you know what a small town is. Everyone got wise to me. They all said I was a no-good tramp. I didn't give a damn what they said. I hated everybody in the place. That is, except Evelyn. I loved Evelyn. Even as a kid. And Evelyn loved me. (*He pauses.*)

No one moves or gives any sign except by the dread in their eyes that they have heard him. Except PARRITT, who takes his hands from his face to look at LARRY pleadingly.

PARRITT. I loved Mother, Larry! No matter what she did! I still do! Even though I know she wishes now I was dead! You believe that, don't you? Christ, why can't you say something?

HICKEY (*too absorbed in his story now to notice this – goes on in a tone of fond, sentimental reminiscence*). Yes, sir, as far back as I can remember, Evelyn and I loved each other. She always stuck up for me. She wouldn't believe the gossip – or she'd pretend she didn't. No one could convince her I was no good. Evelyn was stubborn as all hell once she'd made up her mind. Even when I'd admit things and ask her forgiveness, she'd make excuses for me and defend me against myself. She'd kiss me and say she knew I didn't mean it and I wouldn't do it again. So I'd promise I wouldn't. I'd have to promise, she was so sweet and good, though I knew darned well – (*A touch of strange bitterness comes into his voice for a moment.*) No, sir, you couldn't stop Evelyn. Nothing on earth could shake her faith in me. Even I couldn't. She was a sucker for a pipe dream. (*Then quickly.*) Well, naturally, her family forbid her seeing me. They were one of the town's best, rich for that hick burg, owned the trolley line and lumber company. Strict Methodists, too. They hated my guts. But they couldn't stop Evelyn. She'd sneak notes to me and meet me on the sly. I was getting more restless. The town was getting more like a jail. I made up my mind to beat it. I knew exactly what I wanted to be by that time. I'd met a lot of drummers around the hotel and liked 'em. They were always telling jokes. They were sports. They kept moving. I liked their life. And I knew I could kid people and sell things. The hitch was how to get the railroad fare to the Big Town. I told Mollie Arlington my trouble. She was the madame of the cat-house. She liked me. She laughed and said, 'Hell, I'll stake you, Kid! I'll bet on you. With that grin of yours and that line of bull, you ought to be able to sell skunks for good ratters!' (*He chuckles.*) Mollie was all right. She gave me confidence in myself. I paid her back, the first money I earned. Wrote her a kidding letter, I remember, saying I was peddling baby carriages and she and the girls had better take advantage of our bargain offer. (*He chuckles.*) But that's ahead of my story. The night before I left town, I had a date with Evelyn. I got all worked up, she was so pretty and sweet and good. I told her straight, 'You better forget me Evelyn, for your own sake. I'm no good and never will be. I'm not worthy to wipe your shoes.' I broke down and cried. She just said, looking white and scared, 'Why, Teddy? Don't you still love me?' I said, 'Love you? God, Evelyn, I love you more than anything in the world. And I always will!'

She said, 'Then nothing else matters, Teddy, because nothing but death could stop my loving you. So I'll wait, and when you're ready you send for me and we'll be married. I know I can make you happy, Teddy, and once you're happy you won't want to do any of the bad things you've done any more.' And I said, 'Of course, I won't, Evelyn!' I meant it, too. I believed it. I loved her so much she could make me believe anything. (*He sighs.*)

There is a suspended, waiting silence. Even the two detectives are drawn into it. Then HOPE *breaks into dully exasperated, brutally callous protest.*

HOPE. Get it over, you long-winded bastard! You married her, and you caught her cheating with the iceman, and you croaked her, and who the hell cares? What's she to us? All we want is to pass out in peace, bejees!

A chorus of dull, resentful protest from all the group. They mumble, like sleepers who curse a person who keeps awakening them, 'What's it to us? We want to pass out in peace!' HOPE *drinks and they mechanically follow his example. He pours another and they do the same. He complains with a stupid, nagging insistence.*

No life in the booze! No kick! Dishwater. Bejees, I'll never pass out!

HICKEY (*goes on as if there had been no interruption*). So I beat it to the Big Town. I got a job easy, and it was a cinch for me to make good. I had the knack. I was like a game, sizing people up quick, spotting what their pet pipe dreams were, and then kidding 'em along that line, pretending you believed what they wanted to believe about themselves. They they liked you, they trusted you, they wanted to buy something to show their gratitude. It was fun. But still, all the while I felt guilty, as if I had no right to be having such a good time away from Evelyn. In each letter I'd tell her how I missed her, but I'd keep warning her, too. I'd tell her all my faults, how I liked my booze every once in a while, and so on. But there was no shaking Evelyn's belief in me, or her dreams about the future. After each letter of hers, I'd be as full of faith as she was. So as soon as I got enough saved to start us off, I sent for her and we got married. Christ, wasn't I happy for a while! And wasn't she happy! I don't care what anyone says, I'll bet there never was two people who loved each other more than me and Evelyn. Not only then but always after, in spite of everything I did – (*He pauses – then sadly.*) Well, it's all there, at the start,

everything that happened afterwards. I never could learn to
handle temptation. I'd want to reform and mean it. I'd promise
Evelyn, and I'd promise myself, and I'd believe it. I'd tell her,
it's the last time. And she'd say, 'I know it's the last time,
Teddy. You'll never do it again.' That's what made it so hard.
That's what made me feel such a rotten skunk – her always
forgiving me. My playing around with women, for instance. It
was only a harmless good time to me. Didn't mean anything.
But I'd know what it meant to Evelyn. So I'd say to myself,
never again. But you know how it is, travelling around. The
damned hotel rooms. I'd get seeing things in the wall paper. I'd
get bored as hell. Lonely and homesick. But at the same time
sick of home. I'd feel free and I'd want to celebrate a little. I
never drank on the job, so it had to be dames. Any tart. What
I'd want was some tramp I could be myself with without being
ashamed – someone I could tell a dirty joke to and she'd laugh.

CORA (*with a dull, weary bitterness*). Jees, all de lousy jokes I've
had to listen to and pretend was funny!

HICKEY (*goes on obliviously*). Sometimes I'd try some joke I
thought was a corker on Evelyn. She'd always make herself
laugh. But I could tell she thought it was dirty, not funny. And
Evelyn always knew about the tarts I'd been with when I came
home from a trip. She'd kiss me and look in my eyes, and she'd
know. I'd see in her eyes how she was trying not to know, and
then telling herself even if it was true, he couldn't help it, they
tempt him, and he's lonely, he hasn't got me, it's only his body,
anyway, he doesn't love them, I'm the only one he loves. She
was right, too. I never loved anyone else. Couldn't if I wanted
to. (*He pauses.*) She forgave me even when it all had to come
out in the open. You know how it is when you keep taking
chances. You may be lucky for a long time, but you get nicked
in the end. I picked up a nail from some tart in Altoona.

CORA (*dully, without resentment*). Yeah. And she picked it up from
some guy. It's all in de game. What de hell of it?

HICKEY. I had to do a lot of lying and stalling when I got home.
It didn't do any good. The quack I went to got all my dough
and then told me I was cured and I took his word. But I
wasn't, and poor Evelyn – But she did her best to make me
believe she fell for my lie about how travelling men get things
from drinking-cups on trains. Anyway, she forgave me. The
same way she forgave me every time I'd turn up after a
periodical drunk. You all know what I'd be like at the end of

one. You've seen me. Like something lying in the gutter that no
alley cat would lower itself to drag in – something they threw
out of the DT ward in Bellevue along with the garbage,
something that ought to be dead and isn't! (*His face is convulsed
with self-loathing.*) Evelyn wouldn't have heard from me in a
month or more. She'd have been waiting there alone, with the
neighbours shaking their heads and feeling sorry for her out
loud. That was before she got me to move to the outskirts,
where there weren't any next-door neighbours. And then the
door would open and in I'd stumble – looking like what I've
said – into her home, where she kept everything so spotless and
clean. And I'd sworn it would never happen again, and now I'd
have to start swearing again this was the last time. I could see
disgust having a battle in her eyes with love. Love always won.
She'd make herself kiss me, as if nothing had happened, as if
I'd just come home from a business trip. She'd never complain
or bawl me out. (*He bursts out in a tone of anguish that has anger
and hatred beneath it.*) Christ, can you imagine what a guilty
skunk she made me feel! If she'd only admitted once she didn't
believe any more in her pipe dream that some day I'd behave!
But she never would. Evelyn was stubborn as hell. Once she'd
set her heart on anything, you couldn't shake her faith that it
had to come true – tomorrow! It was the same old story, over
and over, for years and years. It kept piling up, inside her and
inside me. God, can you picture all I made her suffer, and all
the guilt she made me feel, and how I hated myself! If she only
hadn't been so damned good – if she'd been the same kind of
wife I was a husband. God, I used to pray sometimes she'd –
I'd even say to her, 'Go on, why don't you, Evelyn? It'd serve
me right. I wouldn't mind. I'd forgive you.' Of course, I'd
pretend I was kidding – the same way I used to joke here
about her being in the hay with the iceman. She'd have been so
hurt if I'd said it seriously. She'd have thought I'd stopped
loving her. (*He pauses – then looking around at them.*) I suppose
you think I'm a liar, that no woman could have stood all she
stood and still loved me so much – that it isn't human for any
woman to be so pitying and forgiving. Well, I'm not lying, and
if you'd ever seen her, you'd realize I wasn't. It was written all
over her face, sweetness and love and pity and forgiveness. (*He
reaches mechanically for the inside pocket of his coat.*) Wait! I'll show
you. I always carry her picture. (*Suddenly he looks startled. He
stares before him, his hand falling back – quietly.*) No, I'm forgetting
I tore it up – afterwards. I didn't need it any more. (*He pauses.*)

The silence is like that in the room of a dying man where people hold their breath, waiting for him to die.

CORA (*with a muffled sob*). Jees, Hickey! Jees! (*She shivers and puts her hands over her face.*)

PARRITT (*to* LARRY *in a low insistent tone*). I burnt up Mother's picture, Larry. Her eyes followed me all the time. They seemed to be wishing I was dead!

HICKEY. It kept piling up, like I've said. I got so I thought of it all the time. I hated myself more and more, thinking of all the wrong I'd done to the sweetest woman in the world who loved me so much. I got so I'd curse myself for a lousy bastard every time I saw myself in the mirror. I felt such pity for her it drove me crazy. You wouldn't believe a guy like me, that's knocked around so much, could feel such pity. It got so every night I'd wind up hiding my face in her lap, bawling and begging her forgiveness. And of course, she'd always comfort me and say, 'Never mind, Teddy. I know you won't ever again.' Christ, I loved her so, but I began to hate that pipe dream! I began to be afraid I was going bughouse, because sometimes I couldn't forgive her for forgiving me. I even caught myself hating her for making me hate myself so much. There's a limit to the guilt you can feel and the forgiveness and the pity you can take! You have to begin blaming someone else, too. I got so sometimes when she'd kiss me it was like she did it on purpose to humiliate me, as if she'd spit in my face! But all the time I saw how crazy and rotten of me that was and it made me hate myself all the more. You'd never believe I could hate so much, a good-natured, happy-go-lucky slob like me. And as the time got nearer to when I was due to come here for my drunk around Harry's birthday, I got nearly crazy. I kept swearing to her every night that this time I really wouldn't, until I'd made it a real final test to myself – and to her. And she kept encouraging me and saying, 'I can see you really mean it now, Teddy. I know you'll conquer it this time, and we'll be so happy, dear.' When she'd say that and kiss me, I'd believe it, too. Then she'd go to bed, and I'd stay up alone because I couldn't sleep and I didn't want to disturb her, tossing and rolling around. I'd get so damned lonely. I'd get thinking how peaceful it was here, sitting around with the old gang, getting drunk and forgetting love, joking and laughing and singing and swapping lies. And finally I knew I'd have to come. And I knew if I came this time, it was the finish. I'd never have the guts to go back and be forgiven again, and that would break

Evelyn's heart because to her it would mean I didn't love her
any more. (*He pauses.*) That last night, I'd driven myself crazy
trying to figure some way out for her. I went in the bedroom. I
was going to tell her it was the end. But I couldn't do that to
her. She was sound asleep. I thought, God, if she'd only never
wake up, she'd never know! And then it came to me – the only
possible way out, for her sake. I remembered I'd given her a
gun for protection while I was away and it was in the bureau
drawer. She'd never feel any pain, never wake up from her
dream. So I –

HOPE (*tries to ward this off by pounding with his glass on the table –
with brutal, callous exasperation*). Give us a rest, for the love of
Christ! Who the hell cares? We want to pass out in peace!

They all, except PARRITT *and* LARRY, *pound with their glasses
and grumble in chorus:* 'Who the hell cares? We want to pass out
in peace!' MORAN, *the detective, moves quietly from the entrance in
the curtain across the back of the room to the table where his
companion,* LIEB, *is sitting.* ROCKY *notices his leaving and gets up
from the table in the rear and goes back to stand and watch in the
entrance.* MORAN *exchanges a glance with* LIEB, *motioning him to
get up. The latter does so. No one notices them. The clamour of
banging glasses dies out as abruptly as it started.* HICKEY *hasn't
appeared to hear it.*

HICKEY (*simply*). So I killed her.

*There is a moment of dead silence. Even the detectives are caught in it
and stand motionless.*

PARRITT (*suddenly gives up and relaxes limply in his chair – in a low
voice in which there is a strange exhausted relief*). I may as well
confess, Larry. There's no use lying any more. You know,
anyway. I didn't give a damn about the money. It was because I
hated her.

HICKEY (*obliviously*). And then I saw I'd always known that was
the only possible way to give her peace and free her from the
misery of loving me. I saw it meant peace for me, too, knowing
she was at peace. I felt as though a ton of guilt was lifted off
my mind. I remember I stood by the bed and suddenly I had
to laugh. I couldn't help it, and I knew Evelyn would forgive
me. I remember I heard myself speaking to her, as if it was
something I'd always wanted to say: 'Well, you know what you
can do with your pipe dream now, you damned bitch!' (*He stops
with a horrified start, as if shocked out of a nightmare, as if he couldn't
believe he heard what he had just said. He stammers.*) No! I never – !

PARRITT (*to* LARRY – *sneeringly*). Yes, that's it! her and the damned old Movement pipe dream! Eh, Larry?

HICKEY (*bursts into frantic denial*). No! That's a lie! I never said – ! Good God, I couldn't have said that! If I did, I'd gone insane! Why, I loved Evelyn better than anything in life! (*He appeals brokenly to the crowd.*) Boys, you're all my old pals! You've known old Hickey for years! You know I'd never – (*His eyes fix on* HOPE.) You've known me longer than anyone, Harry. You know I must have been insane, don't you, Governor?

HOPE (*at first with the same defensive callousness – without looking at him*). Who the hell cares? (*Then suddenly he looks at* HICKEY *and there is an extraordinary change in his expression. His face lights up, as if he were grasping some dawning hope in his mind. He speaks with a groping eagerness.*) Insane? You mean – you went really insane?

At the tone of his voice, all the group at the tables by him start and stare at him as if they caught his thought. then they all look at HICKEY *eagerly too.*

HICKEY. Yes! Or I couldn't have laughed! couldn't have said that to her!

MORAN *walks up behind him on one side, while the second detective,* LIEB, *closes in on him from the other.*

MORAN (*taps* HICKEY *on the shoulder*). That's enough Hickman. You know who we are. You're under arrest.

He nods to LIEB, *who slips a pair of handcuffs on* HICKEY's *wrists.* HICKEY *stares at them with stupid incomprehension.* MORAN *takes his arm.*

Come along and spill your guts where we can git it on paper.

HICKEY. No, wait Officer! You owe me a break! I phoned and made it easy for you, didn't I? Just a few minutes! (*To* HOPE – *pleadingly.*) You know I couldn't say that to Evelyn, don't you, Harry – unless –

HOPE (*eagerly*). And you've been crazy ever since? Everything you've said and done here –

HICKEY (*for a moment forgets his own obsession and his face takes on its familiar expression of affectionate amusement and he chuckles*). Now, Governor! Up to your old tricks eh? I see what you're driving at, but I can't let you get away with – (*Then, as* HOPE's *expression turns to resentful callousness again and he looks away, he adds hastily with pleading desperation.*) Yes, Harry, of course, I've been out of my mind ever since! All the time I've been here! You saw I was insane, didn't you?

MORAN (*with cynical disgust*). Can it! I've had enough of your act. Save it for the jury. (*Addressing the crowd sharply.*) Listen, you guys. Don't fall for his lies. He's starting to get foxy now and thinks he'll plead insanity. But he can't get away with it.

The crowd at the grouped tables are grasping at hope now. They glare at him resentfully.

HOPE (*begins to bristle in his old-time manner*). Bejees you dumb dick, you've got a crust trying to tell us about Hickey! We've known him for years, and every one of us noticed he was nutty the minute he showed up here! Bejees, if you'd heard all the crazy bull he was pulling about bringing us peace – like a bughouse preacher escaped from an asylum! If you'd seen all the damned fool things he made us do! We only did them because – (*He hesitates – then defiantly.*) Because we hoped he'd come out of it if we kidded him along and humoured him. (*He looks around at the others.*) Ain't that right, fellers?

They burst into a chorus of eager assent: 'Yes, Harry!' 'That's it, Harry!' 'That's why!' 'We knew he was crazy!' 'Just to humour him!'

MORAN. A fine bunch of rats! Covering up for a dirty, cold-blooded murderer.

HOPE (*stung into recovering all his old fuming truculence*). Is that so? Bejees, you know the old story, when Saint Patrick drove the snakes out of Ireland they swam to New York and joined the police force! Ha! (*He cackles insultingly.*) Bejees, we can believe it now when we look at you, can't we, fellers?

They all growl assent, glowering defiantly at MORAN.
MORAN glares at them, looking as if he's like to forget his prisoner and start cleaning out the place. HOPE goes on pugnaciously.

You stand up for your rights, bejees, Hickey! Don't let this smart-aleck dick get funny with you. If he pulls any rubber-hose tricks, you let me know! I've still got friends at the Hall! Bejees, I'll have him back in uniform pounding a beat where the only graft he'll get will be stealing tin cans from the goats!

MORAN (*furiously*). Listen, you cockeyed old bum, for a plugged nickel I'd – (*Controlling himself, turns to* HICKEY, *who is oblivious to all this, and yanks his arm.*) Come on, you!

HICKEY (*with a strange mad earnestness*). Oh, I want to go, Officer.
I can hardly wait now. I should have phoned you from the
house right afterwards. It was a waste of time coming here. I've
got to explain to Evelyn. But I know she's forgiven me. She
knows I was insane. You've got me all wrong, Officer. I want to
go to the Chair.

MORAN. Crap!

HICKEY (*exasperatedly*). God, you're a dumb dick! Do you
suppose I give a damn about life now? Why, you bonehead, I
haven't got a single damned lying hope or pipe dream left!

MORAN (*jerks him around to face the door to the hall*). Get a move
on!

HICKEY (*as they start walking toward rear – insistently*). All I want
you to see is I was out of my mind afterwards, when I laughed
at her! I was a raving rotten lunatic or I couldn't have said –
Why, Evelyn was the only thing on God's earth I ever loved! I'd
have killed myself before I'd ever have hurt her!

They disappear in the hall. HICKEY's voice keeps on protesting.

HOPE (*calls after him*). Don't worry, Hickey! They can't give you
the Chair! We'll testify you was crazy! Won't we, fellers?

*They all assent. Two or three echo HOPE's 'Don't worry, Hickey.'
Then from the hall comes the slam of the street door. HOPE's face falls
– with genuine sorrow.*

He's gone. Poor crazy son of a bitch! (*All the group around him
are sad and sympathetic, too. HOPE reaches for his drink.*) Bejees, I
need a drink. (*They grab their glasses. HOPE says hopefully.*)
Bejees, maybe it'll have the old kick, now he's gone.

He drinks and they follow suit.

ROCKY (*comes forward from where he has stood in the bar entrance –
hopefully*). Yeah, Boss, maybe we can get drunk now. (*He sits in
the chair by CHUCK and pours a drink and tosses it down.*)

*Then they all sit still, waiting for the effect, as if this drink were a
crucial test, so absorbed in hopeful expectancy that they remain
oblivious to what happens at LARRY's table.*

LARRY (*his eyes full of pain and pity – in a whisper, aloud to himself*).
May the Chair bring him peace at last, the poor tortured
bastard!

PARRITT (*leans toward him – in a strange low insistent voice*). Yes,

but he isn't the only one who needs peace, Larry. I can't feel
sorry for him. He's lucky. He's through, now. It's all decided
for him. I wish it was decided for me. I've never been any good
at deciding things. Even about selling out, it was the tart the
detective agency got after me who put it in my mind. You
remember what Mother's like, Larry. She makes all the
decisions. She's always decided what I must do. She doesn't like
anyone to be free but herself. (*He pauses, as if waiting for
comment, but* LARRY *ignores him.*) I suppose you think I ought
to have made those dicks take me away with Hickey. But how
could I prove it, Larry! They'd think I was nutty. Because she's
still alive. You're the only one who can understand how guilty I
am. Because you know her and what I've done to her. You
know I'm really much guiltier than he is. You know what I did
is a much worse murder. Because she is dead and yet she has
to live. For a while. But she can't live long in jail. She loves
freedom too much. And I can't kid myself like Hickey, that
she's at peace. As long as she lives, she'll never be able to forget
what I've done to her even in her sleep. She'll never have a
second's peace. (*He pauses – then bursts out.*) Jesus, Larry, can't
you say something? (LARRY *is at the breaking point.* PARRITT
goes on.) And I'm not putting up any bluff, either, that I was
crazy afterwards when I laughed to myself and thought, 'You
know what you can do with your freedom pipe dream now,
don't you, you damned old bitch!'

LARRY (*snaps and turns on him, his face convulsed with detestation.
His quivering voice has a condemning command in it*). Go! Get the
hell out of life, God damn you, before I choke it out of you!
Go up – !

PARRITT (*his manner is at once transformed. He seems suddenly at
peace with himself. He speaks simply and gratefully*). Thanks, Larry.
I just wanted to be sure. I can see now it's the only possible way
I can ever get free from her. I guess I've really known that all
my life. (*He pauses – then with a derisive smile.*) It ought to
comfort Mother a little too. It'll give her the chance to play the
great incorruptible Mother of the Revolution, whose only child
is the Proletariat. She'll be able to say: 'Justice is done! So may
all traitors die!' She'll be able to say: 'I am glad he's dead! Long
live the Revolution!' (*He adds with a final implacable jeer.*) You
know her, Larry! Always a ham!

LARRY (*pleads distractedly*). Go, for the love of Christ, you mad
tortured bastard, for your own sake!

HUGO *is roused by this. He lifts his head and peers uncomprehendingly at* LARRY. *Neither* LARRY *nor* PARRITT *notices him.*

PARRITT (*stares at* LARRY. *His face begins to crumble as if he were going to break down and sob. He turns his head away, but reaches out fumblingly and pats* LARRY's *arm and stammers*). Jesus, Larry, thanks. That's kind. I knew you were the only one who could understand my side of it. (*He gets to his feet and turns towards the door.*)

HUGO (*looks at* PARRITT *and bursts into his silly giggle*). Hello, leedle Don, leedle monkey-face! Don't be a fool! Buy me a trink!

PARRITT (*puts on an act of dramatic bravado – forcing a grin*). Sure, I will, Hugo! Tomorrow! Beneath the willow trees!

He walks to the door with a careless swagger and disappears in the hall. From now on, LARRY *waits, listening for the sound he knows is coming from the backyard outside the window, but trying not to listen, in an agony of horror and cracking nerve.*

HUGO (*stares after* PARRITT *stupidly*). Stupid fool! Hickey make you crazy, too. (*He turns to the oblivious* LARRY – *with a timid eagerness.*) I'm glad, Larry, they take that crazy Hickey avay to asylum. He makes me have bad dreams. He makes me tell lies about myself. He makes me want to spit on all I have ever dreamed. Yes, I am glad they take him to asylum. I don't feel I am dying now. He vas selling death to me, that crazy salesman. I think I have a trink now, Larry (*He pours a drink and gulps it down.*)

HOPE (*jubilantly*). Bejees, fellers, I'm feeling the old kick, or I'm a liar! It's putting life back in me! Bejees, if all I've lapped up begins to hit me, I'll be paralysed before I know it! It was Hickey kept it from – Bejees, I know that sounds crazy, but he was crazy, and he'd got all of us as bughouse as he was. Bejees, it does queer things to you, having to listen day and night to a lunatic's pipe dreams – pretending you believe them, to kid him along and doing any crazy thing he wants to humour him. It's dangerous, too. Look at me pretending to start fer a walk just to keep him quiet. I knew damned well it wasn't the right day for it. The sun was broiling and the streets full of automobiles. Bejees, I could feel myself getting sunstroke, and an automobile damn near ran over me. (*He appears to* ROCKY, *afraid of the result, but daring it.*) Ask Rocky. He was watching. Didn't it, Rocky?

ROCKY (*a bit tipsily*). What's dat, Boss? Jees, all de booze I've
mopped up is beginning to get to me. (*Earnestly.*) De
automobile, Boss? Sure, I seen it! Just missed yuh! I thought
yuh was a goner. (*He pauses – then looks around at the others, and
assumes the old kidding tone of the inmates, but hesitantly, as if still a
little afraid.*) On de woid of a honest bartender! (*He tries a wink
at the others.*)

They all respond with smiles that are still a little forced and uneasy.

HOPE (*flashes him a suspicious glance. Then he understands – with his
natural testy manner*). You're a bartender, all right. No one can
say different. (ROCKY *looks grateful.*) But, bejees, don't pull
that honest junk! You and Chuck ought to have cards in the
Burglars' Union! (*This time there is an eager laugh from the group,*
HOPE *is delighted.*) Bejees, it's good to hear someone laugh
again! All the time that bas – poor old Hickey was here, I
didn't have the heart – Bejees, I'm getting drunk and glad of
it! (*He cackles and reaches for the bottle.*) Come on, fellers. It's on
the house. (*They pour drinks. They begin rapidly to get drunk now.*
HOPE *becomes sentimental.*) Poor old Hickey! We mustn't hold
him responsible for anything he's done. We'll forget that and
only remember him the way we've always known him before –
the kindest, biggest-hearted guy ever wore shoe leather.

They all chorus hearty sentimental assent: 'That's right, Harry!'
'That's all!' 'Finest fellow!' 'Best scout!' *etc.* HOPE *goes on.*

Good luck to him in Matteawan! Come on, bottoms up!

They all drink. At the table by the window LARRY's *hands grip the
edge of the table. Unconsciously his head is inclined toward the window
as he listens.*

LARRY (*cannot hold back an anguished exclamation*). Christ! Why
don't he – !

HUGO (*beginning to be drunk again – peers at him*). Vhy don't he
what? Don't be a fool! Hickey's gone. He vas crazy. Have a
trink. (*Then as he receives no reply – with vague uneasiness.*) What's
matter vith you, Larry? You look funny. What you listen to out
in backyard, Larry?

CORA *begins to talk in the group at right.*

CORA (*tipsily*). Well, I thank Gawd now me and Chuck did all we
could to humour de poor nut. Jees, imagine us goin' off like we
really meant to get married, when we ain't even picked out a
farm yet!

CHUCK (*eagerly*). Sure ting, Baby. We kidded him we was serious.

JIMMY (*confidently – with a gentle, drunken unction*). I may as well say I detected his condition almost at once. All that talk of his about tomorrow, for example. He had the fixed idea of the insane. It only makes them worse to cross them.

WILLIE (*eagerly*). Same with me, Jimmy. Only I spent the day in the park. I wasn't such a damned fool as to –

LEWIS (*getting jauntily drunk*). Picture my predicament I if *had* gone to the Consulate. The pal of mine there is a humorous blighter. He would have got me a job out of pure spite. So I strolled about and finally came to roost in the park (*He grins with affectionate kidding at* WETJOEN.) And lo and behold, who was on the neighbouring bench but my old battlefield companion, the Boer that walks like a man – who, if the British Government had taken my advice, would have been removed from his fetid kraal on the veldt straight to the baboon's cage at the London Zoo, and little children would now be asking their nurses: 'Tell me, Nana, is that the Boer General, the one with the blue behind?' (*They all laugh uproariously.* LEWIS *leans over and slaps* WETJOEN *affectionately on the knee.*) No offence meant, Piet, old chap.

WETJOEN (*beaming at him*). No offence taken, you tamned Limey! (WETJOEN *goes on – grinningly.*) About a job, I felt the same as you, Cecil.

At the table by the window HUGO *speaks to* LARRY *again.*

HUGO (*with uneasy insistence*). What's matter, Larry? You look scared. What you listen for out there?

But LARRY *doesn't hear, and* JOE *begins talking in the group at right.*

JOE (*with drunken self-assurance*). No, suh, I wasn't fool enough to get in no crap game. Not while Hickey's around. Crazy people puts a jinx on you.

MCGLOIN *is now heard. He is leaning across in front of* WETJOEN *to talk to* ED MOSHER *on* HOPE's *left.*

MCGLOIN (*with drunken earnestness*). I know you saw how it was, Ed. There was no good trying to explain to a crazy guy, but it ain't the right time. You know how getting reinstated is.

MOSHER (*decidedly*). Sure, Mac. The same way with the circus.

The boys tell me the rubes are wasting all their money buying food and times never was so hard. And I never was one to cheat for chicken feed.

HOPE (*looks around him in an ecstasy of bleary sentimental content*). Bejees, I'm cockeyed! Bejees, you're all cockeyed! Bejees, we're all all right! Let's have another!

They pour out drinks. At the table by the window LARRY has unconsciously shut his eyes as he listens. HUGO is peering at him frightenedly now.

HUGO (*reiterates stupidly*). What's matter, Larry? Why you keep eyes shut? You look dead. What you listen for in backyard? (*Then, as LARRY doesn't open his eyes or answer, he gets up hastily and moves away from the table, mumbling with frightened anger.*) Crazy fool! You vas crazy like Hickey! You give me bad dreams too. (*He shrinks quickly past the table where HICKEY had sat to the rear of the group at right.*)

ROCKY (*greets him with boisterous affection*). Hello, dere, Hugo! Welcome to de party!

HOPE. Yes, bejees, Hugo! Sit down! Have a drink! Have ten drinks, bejees!

HUGO (*forgetting LARRY and bad dreams, gives his familiar giggle*). Hello, leedle Harry! Hello, nice, leedle, funny monkey-faces! (*Warming up, changes abruptly to his usual declamatory denunciation.*) Gottamned stupid bourgeois! Soon comes the Day of Judgment! (*They make derisive noises and tell him to sit down. He changes again, giggling good-naturedly, and sits at rear of the middle table.*) Give me ten trinks, Harry. Don't be a fool.

They laugh. ROCKY shoves a glass and bottle at him. The sound of MARGIE's and PEARL's voices is heard from the hall, drunkenly shrill. All of the group turn toward the door as the two appear. They are drunk and look blowsy and dishevelled. Their manner as they enter hardens into a brazen defensive truculence.

MARGIE (*stridently*). Gangway for good good whores!

PEARL. Yeah! And we want a drink quick!

MARGIE (*glaring at ROCKY*). Shake de lead outa your pants, Pimp! A little soivice!

ROCKY (*his black bullet eyes sentimental, his round Wop face grinning welcome*). Well, look who's here! (*He goes to them unsteadily, opening his arms.*) Hello, dere, Sweethearts! Jees, I was beginnin' to worry about yuh, honest! (*He tries to embrace them.*)

They push his arms away, regarding him with amazed suspicion.

PEARL. What kind of a gag is dis?

HOPE (*calls to them effusively*). Come on and join the party, you
broads! Bejees, I'm glad to see you!

*The girls exchange a bewildered glance, taking in the party and the
changed atmosphere.*

MARGIE. Jees, what's come off here?

PEARL. Where's dat louse, Hickey?

ROCKY. De cops got him. He'd gone crazy and croaked his wife.
(*The girls exclaim, 'Jees!' But there is more relief than horror in it.
ROCKY goes on.*) He'll get Matteawan. He ain't responsible.
What he's pulled don't mean nuttin'. So forget dat whore stuff.
I'll knock de block off anyone calls you whores! I'll fill de
bastard full of lead! Yuh're tarts, and what de hell of it? Yuh're
as good as anyone! So forget it, see?

*They let him get his arms around them now. He gives them a hug. All
the truculence leaves their faces. They smile and exchange maternally
amused glances.*

MARGIE (*with a wink*). Our little bartender, ain't he, Poil?

PEARL. Yeah, and a cute little Ginny at dat!

They laugh.

MARGIE. And is he stinko!

PEARL. Stinko is right. But he ain't got nuttin' on us. Jees,
Rocky, did we have a big time at Coney!

HOPE. Bejees, sit down, you dumb broads! Welcome home!
Have a drink! Have ten drinks, bejees!

*They take the empty chair on CHUCK's left, warmly welcomed by all.
ROCKY stands in back of them, a hand on each of their shoulders,
grinning with proud proprietorship. HOPE beams over and under his
crooked spectacles with the air of a host whose party is a huge success,
and rambles on happily.*

Bejees, this is all right! We'll make this my birthday party, and
forget the other. We'll get paralysed! But who's missing?
Where's the Old Wise Guy? Where's Larry?

ROCKY. Over by de window, Boss. Jees, he's got his eyes shut.
De old bastard's asleep. (*They turn to look. ROCKY dismisses him.*)
Aw, to hell wid him. Let's have a drink.

They turn away and forget him.

LARRY (*torturedly arguing to himself in a shaken whisper*). It's the only way out for him! For the peace of all concerned, as Hickey said! (*Snapping.*) God damn his yellow soul, if he doesn't soon, I'll go up and throw him off! – like a dog with its guts ripped out you'd put out of misery!

He half rises from his chair just as from outside the window comes the sound of something hurtling down, followed by a muffled, crunching thud . LARRY gasps and drops back on his chair, shuddering, hiding his face in his hands. The group at right hear it but are too preoccupied with drinks to pay much attention.

HOPE (*wonderingly*). What the hell was that?

ROCKY. Aw, nuttin', Something fell off de fire escape. A mattress, I'll bet. Some of dese bums been sleepin' on de fire escapes.

HOPE (*his interest diverted by this excuse to beef – testily*). They've got to cut it out! Bejees, this ain't a fresh air cure. Mattresses cost money.

MOSHER. Now don't start crabbing at the party, Harry. Let's drink up.

HOPE *forgets it and grabs his glass, and they all drink.*

LARRY (*in a whisper of horrified pity*). Poor devil! (*A long-forgotten faith returns to him for a moment and he mumbles.*) God rest his soul in peace. (*He opens his eyes – with a bitter self-derision.*) Ah, the damned pity – the wrong kind, as Hickey said! Be God, there's no hope! I'll never be a success in the grandstand – or anywhere else! Life is too much for me! I'll be a weak fool looking with pity at the two sides of everything till the day I die! (*With an intense bitter sincerity.*) May that day come soon! (*He pauses startledly, surprised at himself – then with a sardonic grin.*) Be God, I'm the only real convert to death Hickey made here. From the bottom of my coward's heart I mean that now!

HOPE (*calls effusively*). Hey there, Larry! Come over and get paralysed! What the hell you doing, sitting there? (*Then as LARRY doesn't reply he immediately forgets him and turns to the party. They are all very drunk now, just a few drinks ahead of the passing-out stage, and hilariously happy about it.*) Bejees, let's sing! Let's celebrate! It's my birthday party! Bejees, I'm orey-eyed! I want to sing!

He starts the chorus 'She's the Sunshine of Paradise Alley,' and instantly they all burst into song. But not the same song. Each starts the chorus of his or her choice. JIMMY TOMORROW'*s is 'A Wee Dock and Doris';* ED MOSHER'*s 'Break the News to Mother';* WILLIE OBAN'*s, the Sailor Lad ditty he sang in Act One;* GENERAL WETJOEN'*s 'Waiting at the Church';* MCGLOIN'*s 'Tammany';* CAPTAIN LEWIS'*s, 'The Old Kent Road';* JOE'*s 'All I Got Was Sympathy';* PEARL'*s and* MARGIE'*s, 'Everybody's Doing It';* ROCKY'*s, 'You Great Big Beautiful Doll';* CHUCK'*s, 'The Curse of an Aching Heart';* CORA'*s, 'The Oceana Roll'; while* HUGO *jumps to his feet and, pounding on the table with his fist, bellows in his guttural basso the French Revolutionary 'Carmagnole.' A weird cacophony results from this mixture and they stop singing to roar with laughter. All but* HUGO, *who keeps on with drunken fervour.*

HUGO. 'Dansons la Carmagnole!
   Vive le son! Vive le son!
   Dansons la Carmagnole!
   Vive le son des canons!'

They all turn on him and howl him down with amused derision. He stops singing to denounce them in his most fiery style.

Capitalist svine! Stupid Bourgeois monkeys! (*He declaims.*) 'The days grow hot, O Babylon!'

They all take it up and shout in enthusiastic jeering chorus.

''Tis cool beneath thy willow trees!'

They pound their glasses on the table, roaring with laughter, and HUGO *giggles with them. In his chair by the window,* LARRY *stares in front of him, oblivious to their racket.*

Curtain.